# VISION
## OF THE
# TEMPLE

**1** Synagogue of Dura-Europos, central niche (Damascus, Damascus Museum)

# VISION
## OF THE
# TEMPLE

## THE IMAGE OF THE TEMPLE OF JERUSALEM IN JUDAISM AND CHRISTIANITY

## Helen Rosenau

ORESKO BOOKS LTD·LONDON

## ACKNOWLEDGEMENTS

The publisher's sincere thanks are due to the following for their help in providing photographs and in giving permission for these to be reproduced: Agnew's, London; Archives Municipales, Bordeaux; Austrian National Tourist Office, London; Dr. R.D. Barnett; Biblioteca Nacional, Madrid; Bibliothèque Nationale, Paris; Bibliothèque Publique et Universitaire, Geneva; Bischöfliches Bauamt, Würzburg; Bodleian Library, Oxford; Boymans-van Beuningen Museum, Rotterdam; Brandeis University, Waltham, Massachusetts; Brera Gallery, Milan; British Library, London; British Museum, London; Charleston Trident Chamber of Commerce, Charleston; Damascus National Museum, Damascus; Hermitage Museum, Leningrad; Israel Department of Antiquities and Museums, Jerusalem; Israel Exploration Society, Jerusalem; Israel Government Tourist Office, London; Israel Museum, Jerusalem; Jewish Museum, New York; Jewish Theological Seminary, New York; Keter Publishing House, Ltd., Jerusalem; Rabbi Bernard Lipnick, Congregation B'nai Amoona, St. Louis; Mauritshuis, The Hague; Monumenti Musei e Gallerie Pontificie, Vatican; Musée des Beaux-Arts, Caen; Musée du Louvre, Paris; Musée National Message Biblique, Nice; Museum für Hamburgische Geschichte, Hamburg; National Gallery of Scotland, Edinburgh; Netherlands National Tourist Office, London; Portuguese-Israeli Community, Rotterdam; Royal Library, Copenhagen; Sarajevo Museum, Sarajevo; Mr. Alexander Scheiber, Dohany Ucca Temple, Budapest; Semper-Archiv, Zürich; Service de Documentation Photographique de la Réunion des Musées Nationaux, Paris; Staatgeschichtliches Museum, Düsseldorf; Staatgeschichtliches Museum, Nördlingen; Topkapi Museum, Istanbul; University Museum of Jena, Jena; Victoria and Albert Museum, London; Yale University Art Gallery, New Haven; A.D.A.G.P., Paris (Illus. 149); Alinari, Florence; Erich Andres, Hamburg; Jean Arlaud, Geneva; G.L.W. Oppenheim, Amsterdam; H.E. Müller, Hamburg.

First published in Great Britain by
Oresko Books Ltd., 30 Notting Hill Gate, London W11

UK ISBN 0905368 24 X

Printed and Bound in England by JB Offset Printers (Marks Tey) Ltd.

# Contents

Foreword                                                                7

Preface and Acknowledgements                                            9

Glossary/Abbreviations                                                 11

Introduction                                                           13

Chapter I: Antiquity, Destruction and Spiritual Survival              19
*illustration 1, page 2; illustration 2, page 6; illustrations 3–15,
pages 26–31*

Chapter II: Abstract Design and Structural Vision                     32
*illustration 16, page 32; illustrations 17–51, pages 45–63*

Chapter III: Aspects of Realism                                       64
*illustration 52, page 64; illustrations 53–80, pages 70–89*

Chapter IV: Reformation and Counter-Reformation                      90
*illustration 81, page 90; illustrations 82–119, pages 101–131*

Chapter V: Contributions to the Baroque and the Enlightenment       132
*illustrations 120 and 121, page 132; illustrations 122–147,
pages 143–159*

Chapter VI: Past Concepts and Future Trends                         160
*illustration 148, page 160; illustrations 149–163, pages 168–179*

Conclusions                                                         180
*illustration 164, page 180; illustrations 165 and 166, page 183*

Extracts from Sources                                               184

Select Bibliography                                                 187

Index                                                              189

2  Arch of Titus, Rome, interior bas relief showing the spoils of Jerusalem (photo, Alinari)

# Foreword

DR. HELEN ROSENAU is a distinguished art scholar and historian whose work *Boullée and Architectural Vision*, published in 1974, is a sensitive study, lavishly and beautifully illustrated, which delineates how men and societies have reacted to what she calls 'architectural vision'. In the present volume, *Vision of the Temple*, she has turned her attention, within an astringent discipline of the same method and basic approach, to another symbol not entirely unrelated to her former volume. Certainly in its emotive, aesthetic and religious connotations, the theme which she now undertakes deserves attention not least in a study of this kind. What Dr. Rosenau does is to see how the Temple, with a historic locus in Jerusalem, yet not confined to Judaism but found as a symbol and reality in other faiths, has fired the imagination and authenticated something precious to man's religious awareness. 'The convergence between the concept of the Temple and the Tabernacle can here be observed, demonstrating how the Temple became increasingly a universal symbol, no longer connected with a single site or one religious viewpoint.' Here is the nub of her thesis which a wide-ranging scholarship illuminates. True, in the Book of the *Revelation* it says: 'I saw no temple therein'; but this negative, paradoxically, is itself testimony to the significance of the sacred building so long as mankind is *in via*. The Jewish community has thought in terms of Solomon's Temple and the accompaniments of its worshipful use. Christian mythology is also rich in its Temple symbolism but has looked to its historical delineation in the Book of *Chronicles*. Behind and interpenetrating Dr. Rosenau's study there is the deep conviction of the need for man to revere his holy buildings, that is buildings set apart, not to 'desacralize' the secular but to enrich it. So the Temple may be taken as representative of a far wider universe of discourse than its visible historic embodiment. Dr. Johnson, recollecting in tranquillity his dangerous journey in an open boat until he finally alighted on the island of Iona, wrote: 'The man is little to be envied whose patriotism would not gain force upon the plains of Marathon, or whose piety would not grow warmer among the ruins of Iona'. Dr. Johnson has made a name as shrewd and commonsensical; and here he is registering an emotion endemic in the depths of our common human nature. A book such as Dr. Rosenau's, with its refined scholarship and insight, comes well at a time when buildings seem often to be written off in religious circles and their deeper symbolism forgotten. We do this to our own impoverishment.

I commend warmly Helen Rosenau's *Vision of the Temple*.

Edward Carpenter
Dean of Westminster

# Preface and Acknowledgements

THE SUBJECT DISCUSSED in this study is vast and connected with many different periods and civilizations. Complete coverage of all existing material, therefore, was neither possible nor intended, the emphasis being on western European developments, but it is hoped that the essential steps in the evolution of the Temple image have been traced. It has to be appreciated that the religious and aesthetic interest in the subject varied throughout history and, therefore, the ensuing chapters are unequal in length. Without the help of libraries, museums, scholars and friends, who cannot all be named, the task would have been impossible.

I particularly desire to thank the Very Rev. Dr. Edward Carpenter, Dean of Westminster, for his foreword. It is rare indeed for writers to meet such sympathetic understanding, which is bound to give great encouragement.

I wish to thank the authorities of the Bodleian Library, Oxford; the British Library, the British Museum and the Jews' College, London; the John Rylands Library, Manchester; the Archives Nationales, Paris; the Archives Municipales, Bordeaux; both the Manuscript Department and the Print Room at the Bibliothèque Nationale, Paris; the Rosenthaliana University Library, Amsterdam; the Judaica Section, Royal Library, Copenhagen; the Wiener Library, London; and the Jewish Claims Conference, for an initial research grant. I also wish to express my thanks to M. François Avril, who kindly supplied a descriptive list of Nicolaus de Lyra manuscripts.

I desire to record my gratitude for valuable suggestions made by Professor Busink, Dr. D. L. Douie, M. and Mme. Gallet, Rabbi Dr. David Goldstein, Mr. L. Hoffman, Dr. C. R. Ligota, Miss A. de la Mare, Mr. R. A. May, M. and Mme. Metzger, Mr. D. L. Paisey, Professor F.-G. Pariset, Dr. D. Patterson, Rabbi J. D. Rayner, Mrs. Marian Rickards, Dr. I. Schachar, Mr. E. Silver, Mr. P. Slater, Dr. B. Smalley and the designer Richard Kelly. Mr. K. E. Wilson was kind enough to assist in completing the typescript. My publisher, Robert Oresko, has sustained his

9

interest in my work with great integrity and thoughtfulness, and I want to thank him. I wish to conclude with a translation from the *Ethics of the Fathers* found in the *Mishnah* (*Aboth* II:16): 'You are not required to complete the work, but neither are you at liberty to abstain.'

H.R. 1976

Reference to publications since 1977 could not be included in this study. Therefore a discussion of the architectural descriptions in the *Temple Scroll* found in Professor Yigael Yadin's Hebrew edition of 1977 and the summary by Professor Jacob Milgrom in *Biblical Archeologist,* vol. 41 (1978), has to be postponed for another occasion.

H.R. 1979

# Glossary/Abbreviations

**Aboth** (or 'fathers')  Book of the *Talmud* (q.v.) referring to ethics

**Altar of the Holocaust**  Altar for burnt offerings, in the forecourt of the Tabernacle and of the Temple

**Ark of the Covenant**  Ark in the Holy of Holies (q.v.) containing only the Tablets of the Law

**Avodah Zarah** (or 'worship of "strange gods" or idols')  Book of the *Talmud* (q.v.)

**Baba Bathra** (or 'the last gate')  Book of the *Talmud* (q.v.)

**Chanukka**  Festival in commemoration of the re-dedication of the Temple

**Dome of the Rock**  Mosque on Mount Moriah, the Temple Mount (q.v.)

**Haggadah**  Story of the Exodus, recited at Passover

**Hall of the Forest of Lebanon**  Monumental building constructed by Solomon for an uncertain purpose

**Holy of Holies**  Part of the Tabernacle and of the Temple which was the traditional resting place of the Ark with the Tablets of the Law until the Babylonian Exile

**Masoretic, Masorah**  Method of writing Hebrew biblical text

**Megillah**  Scroll of Esther

**Menahoth** (or 'meal offering')  Book of the *Talmud* (q.v.)

**Menorah**  Seven-branch candlestick of the Tabernacle and the Temple.

**Mesibbah**  Winding passage

**Middoth** (or 'measurements')  Tractate of the *Mishnah* (q.v.) on the Temple architecture

**Midrash**   Scriptural exegesis or homiletics

**Mishnah** (or Mischna)   Constituent part, with the *Gemara*, of the *Talmud* (q.v.), the post-Mosaic compilation of Jewish law

**Palace of Solomon**   Structure built on the Temple Mount (q.v.) to the south of the Temple

**Shrine for the Scrolls**   Holy receptacle in the synagogue equivalent to the Ark

**Sukkah** (or 'booth')   Book of the *Talmud* (q.**v.**) referring to the Feast of Tabernacles

**Synagogue**   Jewish place of worship, subsidiary to the Temple until the destruction of the latter

**Tabernacle**   Holy Tent in the wilderness

**Talmud** (or 'teaching')   Body of Jewish law and legend comprising the *Mishnah* (precepts of the elders, codified c. A.D. 200 with older material) and the *Gemara* (commentary on the *Mishnah*) dating in the Palestine *Talmud* from c. A.D. 400 and in the Babylonian *Talmud,* a fuller version, from c. A.D. 500

**Temple Mount**   Large hill on which the Temple was built, traditionally where the sacrifice of Isaac was to have taken place and the site of Ornan's threshing floor, where David raised an altar to the Lord

**Torah** (or 'instruction', incorrectly translated as 'law')   Five Books of Moses, or Pentateuch, in which the Divine Will is revealed

## ABBREVIATIONS

*Baron:* Baron, I. W., *A Social and Religious History of the Jews.* New York 1952 etc.
*Hollis:* Hollis, F. J., *The Archaeology of Herod's Temple.* London 1934.
*Rosenau, Jewish Art:* Rosenau, H., *A Short History of Jewish Art.* London 1948.
*Rosenau, The Ideal City:* Rosenau, H., *The Ideal City: its Architectural Evolution.* (2nd edn.) London 1974.
*Thieme-Becker:* Thieme, U. and Becker, F., *Allgemeines Lexikon der bildenden Künstler von der Antike bis zur Gegenwart.* Leipzig 1907 etc.
*Wischnitzer, The European Synagogue:* Wischnitzer, R., *The Architecture of the European Synagogue.* Philadelphia 1964.
*Wischnitzer, Synagogue Architecture in the United States:* Wischnitzer, R., *Synagogue Architecture in the United States: History and Interpretation.* Philadelphia 1955.

# Introduction

'The heaven and heaven of heavens cannot contain thee;
how much less this house that I have built?'
I *Kings* 8: 27

THE HISTORY OF art deals on occasions with persistent architectural images, which, because of their religious symbolism and connotations, inspire continuous re-interpretation and rediscovery. The most significant among these is, perhaps, the image of the Jewish Temple in Jerusalem, which represents a focus of religious emotion for both Judaism and Christianity. It is a subject which illumines stylistic change whilst retaining iconographic continuity. It is, therefore, worth studying both for its own sake and as a historical sequence. Obviously, Temple illustrations are extremely numerous, and it is attempted here to deal with only outstanding examples.

The image of the Temple, however, also illustrates the complex relationship between Jews and Christians, an ambivalent attitude which, as far as Christians were concerned, alternated between persecution and respect, disdain and consultation. Jews were victims as well as teachers and endeavoured to keep aloof from their persecutors, although individual cases of Judaeo-Christian friendship are recorded. These, however, were based mainly on exchanges of views between scholars and failed to influence the beliefs of the masses, society remaining largely intolerant in spite of political change.

This study attempts the elucidation of iconographic problems regarding the visual image of the Temple and aims at an aesthetic appreciation of the formal structure that inspired the pictorial tradition. It should be remembered that the word *templum* in its original Latin meaning defines a measured sacred space, either on earth or in heaven.[1] The relationship to a house that is the habitation of the god and includes his cult image is secondary. *Templum* is therefore not equivalent to the Hebrew designations for the dwellings of God, which are either not described at all, such as a habitation, *naveh* (*Exodus* 15: 13), or among others are specified as a place, *makom* (*Genesis* 28: 17; II *Samuel* 6: 17, in which *makom* is a place within the tent), a tent, *chal* (*Exodus* 29: 44), a tabernacle, *mishkan* (*Exodus* 25: 9; *Psalms* 46: 5) or a house, *bayit* (I *Kings*, *passim*). The term for the holy part, *heikhal*, is sometimes substituted for the whole of the Temple and includes the Holy of Holies, the *debir*.

The holy building is derived architecturally from a divine pattern revealing the shape of the Tabernacle, *tabnit* (*Exodus* 25: 9), and the Temple (I *Chronicles* 28: 11). God's guidance is implied in David's rejection (II *Samuel* 7: 5, 13; I *Chronicles* 17: 12) and the choice of his son Solomon as a builder.

Characteristic of the Jewish Temple's design throughout its history is the emphasis on the longitudinal direction, leading from the entrance through the House to the Holy of Holies, the dwelling place of God in the Ark of the Covenant. This arrangement has, by and large, been adopted by the synagogue, the Shrine of the Scrolls taking the place of the Ark. The sense of longitudinal direction also characterizes the main development of Christian churches in western Europe[2] although, especially in Byzantium and during the early Romanesque period and the Renaissance, a countervailing emphasis on the central plan came to the fore. In Judaism such artistic tendencies also developed, perhaps fostered by the shape of the Moslem Dome of the Rock on the Temple site, although pictorial examples of the centrally-planned Temple are not typical.

*ILL. 3*

Jewish as well as Christian architecture is based on a dynamic religious experience, emphasizing a goal, and forms a contrast to buildings of the mandala type that stress complete enclosure. This is perhaps most convincingly expressed in architectural form by the Pantheon in Rome, a pantheistic interpretation of balanced devotion. By contrast, Jewish and Christian modes of worship are basically allied rather than at variance, and this may be a contributing but by no means the only reason for the evolution of the Jewish Temple as a religious symbol for Christianity and for ecclesiastical architecture.

The Jewish Temple differed from pagan temples in principle by not containing a cult image.[3] This fact is universally recognized, although interpretations with regard to other fittings of the Jewish Temple vary. According to the Bible, Solomon's Temple contained the Ark, reminiscent of the Tabernacle, whilst the Second and Third Temples seem to have had an empty Holy of Holies. For the purpose of this study the modern critical approach to the biblical narrative is irrelevant, as we are dealing here with the established tradition and its influence on visual images; for example, the question whether the texts that describe the Tabernacle and its settings were based on the description of Solomon's Temple or vice versa becomes immaterial in this context.

General agreement on the design of Solomon's Temple has been reached on only a few facts. According to I *Kings* 6: 2, 3, 20, the building was divided into three parts: the porch, or *ulam*, twenty cubits* long and ten cubits wide, which appeared, according to *Middoth* IV: 7, in the time of Herod as a sort of transept, broader at the front than at the back, 'like a lion'; the House proper, the *heikhal*, sixty cubits long, twenty cubits wide and thirty cubits high; and the Holy of Holies, the *debir*, a cube of twenty cubits, included in the length mentioned for the *heikhal*. According to II *Chronicles* 3: 4 the height of the porch was 120 cubits, a measurement twice the length of the House, and in the same spirit of aggrandizement the height of the two free-standing pillars, called Jachin and Boaz, is changed from eighteen cubits recorded in I *Kings* 7: 15 to the thirty-five cubits cited in II *Chronicles* 3: 15.[4]

This tradition of aggrandizement is brushed aside by present-day scholarship as erroneous, although the text of *Chronicles* was regarded as authoritative in the past and repeated not only by Josephus but also earlier by the Judaeo-Greek writer Eupolemos.[5] It is not unreasonable to assume that the biblical chronicler wished the Temple to emulate the sumptuous buildings of the Egyptians and the Babylonians in his description and, therefore, he envisaged some sort of pylon effect or monumental gateway.

Solomon's Temple was reconstructed by Zerubbabel and was followed, in turn, by Herod's ambitious plan. The latter was situated asymmetrically within a square court, the Court of the Israelites, preceded by the Court of Women, which was in turn subdivided into four smaller square and un-roofed sections (*Middoth* II: 5), the area as a whole comprising 500 square cubits (*Middoth* II: 1). 'The greatest area on the south, second to it that on the east and third that on the north, and the least on the west. The area that was of the greatest extent was where there was the greatest amount of traffic'. The exact location of Herod's Temple on the mount is unknown. Hollis suggests the ancient rock, now inside the Dome of the Rock, as the site of the *debir*, although other scholars think that the altar of the forecourt stood on the rock, while Busink assumes that the building was situated more to the north.[6] Naturally enough, the more formal architectural problems and dispositions of the Temple were of little concern to the writers of the *Talmud* and, consequently, topographical details are not included. Similarly, the exact site of Solomon's palace is unknown. The Bible suggests that the palace was sumptuous, as Solomon's Temple took seven years to complete but his palace consumed thirteen years of building (I *Kings* 6: 38; 7: 1). It seems certain, however, that when Herod built the Temple, Solomon's palace had been destroyed.

*A cubit equalled approximately 45·7 cm.

Herod's Temple built of marble was appreciated from an aesthetic point of view. 'He who has not seen the Temple of Herod has never in his life seen a beautiful building' recorded the Babylonian *Talmud* (*Baba Bathra*). After the destruction of Herod's Temple in A.D. 70, there was one attempt, the last, to rebuild the Temple, by the Emperor Julian, popularly known as the Apostate, in 362–63. It is much to be regretted that we do not know more about the emperor's project for the rebuilding, plans that could not have appealed to the Jews since the rebuilding had been associated by then with the Messianic age.[7]

It is likely that the ancient rock, now the central feature of the Moslem Dome of the Rock, was the site of an ancient cult. It is associated in Jewish legend with the sacrifice of Isaac, the *akedah*, and thus expresses redemption. The site surrounding the mount is in process of being excavated and so far a number of significant discoveries have been made referring to the precincts of Herod, in particular to a bridge and stepped walkway as well as traces of a colonnade,[8] thus giving some idea of the *ILL. 161* splendour of Herod's scheme. Archaeology has taken over from the visionary reconstruction, yet within the scientific approach the flame of vision is not extinguished.

Certain basic architectural relationships are expressed in the Bible, such as the cube of the Temple's Holy of Holies, the longitudinal direction and the 'orientation' of the doors to the east, the Ark facing the west. The idea of the Tabernacle in the Wilderness was incorporated in the Temple concept, a fixed abode for the deity taking the place of a movable sanctuary, the holy tent being replaced by a 'house of prayer for all peoples' (*Isaiah* 56: 7).

The Jewish attitude to religious architecture was positive and unambiguous, although pictorial decoration was made difficult in varying degrees by the ancient prohibition of the Second Commandment. This commandment (*Exodus* 20: 4; *Deuteronomy* 5: 8) against the making of images was part of the fight against idolatry and tended to lapse with the defeat of paganism, although the synagogue never went as far as the church in permitting images.[9]

The idea of God inspiring the design was suggested for the Tabernacle as well as for the Temple (*Exodus* 25: 9; I *Chronicles* 28: 11) and is also reflected in mediaeval Christian legend. A story is related of the founding of Santa Maria Maggiore by Pope Liberius, who drew the ground plan of the future church on the site that was indicated to him during a miraculous snowfall on the night of 4–5 August 352.[10] The Temple vision represents a paradox, a building located on a particular site but also a place which was increasingly regarded as a universal and transcending symbol.

The synagogue was probably first established during the existence of the Temple as a hall of religious assembly. It slowly assumed most of the latter's functions, except those connected with ritual sacrifices, after the destruction of Herod's Temple by the Romans in A.D. 70. Both Temple and synagogue were increasingly regarded as holy buildings, and the Temple image, therefore, could be adapted to the concept of the synagogue as a sacred structure, becoming also a prototype for the church. In this sense both *ecclesia* and *synagoga* are derived from the Temple. Iconographically and stylistically the Temple and synagogue pictures in Antiquity are interrelated, exemplifying in this manner the intimate relationship between the two structures. The hope of rebuilding the Temple was expressed especially in the tractate *Aboth* (V: 20) of the Babylonian *Talmud*, stating that Rabbi Judah ben Tema mentioned the rebuilding of the city of Jerusalem. In the Palestinian *Talmud*, it is the rebuilding of the sanctuary itself which is mentioned. Even more interesting is the reference in *Sukkah* (41a and b), in which the speed of the rebuilding of the Temple and even its implications for food consumption are discussed in realistic detail.

The sanctity of the synagogue, 'the little sanctuary' (*Ezekiel* 11: 16), was suggested in Talmudic times, especially in *Bab. Megillah* (29a)[11]. The idea of the holiness of the synagogue was also expressed in Antique inscriptions, including those of the Synagogue of Stobi, presumably of the fourth century A.D., in the Synagogue of Hammam-Lif of the fifth century and in the Synagogue of Na'aran, probably also of the fifth century.[12] However, although the religious significance of the synagogue advanced through the centuries—what happened in the contemporary period will be discussed later—the concept of the Temple remained of unique and transcendent significance.

### References

1   For Jewish references consult throughout L. A. Mayer, *Bibliography of Jewish Art* (ed. O. Kurz) (Jerusalem 1967). Consult also *The Jewish Encyclopedia* (New York and London) and *Encyclopaedia Judaica* under the headings 'Tabernacle' and 'Temple', with bibliographies. For general surveys from a variety of points of view see H. Graetz, *Geschichte der Juden* etc. (first published from 1855 onward in Leipzig; English translation, *History of the Jews*, London and Philadelphia 1891–92); S. Dubnow, *Die Weltgeschichte des Jüdischen Volkes* (Berlin 1925–29; English translation, *History of the Jews,* New Brunswick 1967); I. W. Baron, *A Social and Religious History of the Jews* (New York 1952 etc.) together with H. H. Ben-Sasson (ed.), *A History of the Jewish People* (London 1976); also, for a popular survey, Joan Comay, *The Temple of Jerusalem* (New York 1975). On the *templum* cf. J. Rykwert, *The Idea of a Town* (London 1976).

2   H. Rosenau, *Design and Mediaeval Architecture* (London 1934), *passim*.

3   E. Bevan, *Holy Images* (London 1940); E. R. Goodenough, *Jewish Symbols in the Greco-Roman Period* (New York 1953–65), especially vol. XII. J. Gutmann (ed.), *No Graven Images* (New York 1971) is marginal to our subject; it comprises numerous articles, some of which contain profound analyses of the problems concerned.

4   Hollis, *passim.*

5   T. A. Busink, *Der Tempel von Jerusalem von Salomo bis Herodes* (Leiden 1970), vol. I, p. 166, is typical of this attitude. For a detailed entry, see *Encyclopaedia Judaica* under the heading 'Eupolemus'; also, for background, J. Ouellette in *The Temple of Solomon* (ed. J. Gutmann) (Missoula 1976), pp. 1 ff.

6   Busink, *op. cit.*, pp. 99 ff.

7   See S. P. Brock in *Palestine Exploration Quarterly* (1976), pp. 103 ff.

8   *Qadmoniot*, vol. V (1972), nos. 3–4; Y. Yadin (ed.), *Jerusalem Revealed, Archaeology in the Holy City 1968–74* (New Haven and London 1976), *passim.*

9   See note 3 above.

10   See Rosenau, *op. cit., passim.*

11   S. Krauss, *Synagogale Altertümer* (original edition, Berlin and Vienna 1922; photographic reproduction, Hildesheim 1966) and I. Elbogen, *Der jüdische Gottesdienst in seiner geschichtlichen Entwicklung* (original edition, Berlin 1905; photographic reproduction, Hildesheim 1962) are still indispensable.

12   E. L. Sukenik, *Ancient Synagogues in Palestine and Greece* (London 1934).

CHAPTER I

# Antiquity, Destruction and Spiritual Survival

THE JEWISH TEMPLE has, for many generations, attracted the attention not only of scholars and others interested in the Bible but also of archaeologists and artists. It should be recalled that three successive buildings have to be distinguished in the history of the architecture of the Temple in Jerusalem. The First Temple was built by King Solomon some time between 965 and 928 B.C., the second was the restoration by Zerubbabel about 500 B.C., about which little is known, and the third was erected by Herod I (73 B.C.–A.D. 4) and was destroyed by the Romans in A.D. 70.[1]

The entire tradition covers many centuries and is not without contradictions, for earlier texts are reflected in I *Kings*, written in approximately 550 B.C., and in II *Chronicles*, probably fourth century B.C.

The visions of *Ezekiel* 40–41, probably 593–571 B.C., may well be based on an existing ground plan rather than on an inspection of the irregular site itself. However, a visionary element is paramount, especially with regard to the pure waters springing from the east and flowing south (*Ezekiel* 47: 1). It should be remembered that ground plans were known in Egypt and Babylonia and, although architectural sections and elevations were a later development, models existed for sculptural friezes and shrines. The best surviving example of the ground plan of a temple precinct, held by Gudea on his knees, dates from c. 2000 B.C. and is now in the Louvre, while the plan of the city of Nippur (c. 1500 B.C.) is in the University Museum of Jena.[2]

*ILLS. 4, 5*
*ILL. 6*

Two further textual sources must be added: the description found in *Middoth*, a part of the *Mishnah* (c. A.D. 150) including sayings by Eliezer ben Jacob before Herod's Temple was destroyed, and the description in Josephus's *The Jewish War*, dating from the second half of the first century A.D.[3] It should be remembered that for the purpose of the present study questions of biblical textual criticism do not apply. The writers concerned were selective in their approach to the past and took from tradition what they regarded as important. For them the text was based on revelation, but a critical assessment of sources was not necessarily

completely ruled out. It was only during the post-Renaissance period
that the problem of exactitude in a scientific sense arose.

The image of the Temple first appeared in visual form on the obverse
of some coins after the destruction of Herod's building, testifying to the
longing for its preservation and depicting a vision rather than a reality.
The earliest Temple representations are found on the coins of Bar
Kochba, leader of the Jewish revolt in A.D. 132–135 against the Emperor
Hadrian, and they therefore are associated with the Messianic hopes that
centred upon Bar Kochba.[4] These coins show the front of a building with        *ILL. 7*
a flat roof, supported by four columns or half-columns, and combine an
exterior view of the façade with an opening revealing an object standing on
four supports and surmounted by a semicircular cover. There can be
little doubt that the building stands for the Herodian Temple, within which
appears the Ark of the Covenant. The flat roof, typical of Near Eastern
architecture, is implied in *Middoth* IV: 6, which refers to spikes placed on
the roof to discourage roosting birds. These may perhaps be suggested by
a wavy line at the top of the design on some of the coins. On others
there is a star over the building, referring to Bar Kochba's name, 'son of a
star'. The combination of views found on these coins was not unusual.
It was, indeed, customary on Roman coins for the central supports of a
colonnade to be omitted in order to reveal the cult object within the
temple. In this respect the Bar Kochba coins follow the Roman artistic      *ILL. 10*
tradition.

In 1936 the present writer had already drawn attention to the similarity
of the Bar Kochba coins to the painting crowning the niche for the Scrolls
in the Synagogue of Dura-Europos (completed in A.D. 244–245).[5] It is
well known that the Synagogue of Dura-Europos was fully decorated by     *ILL. 1*
wall paintings which represent a sequence of biblical cycles. This is all
the more important as Dura-Europos was a provincial outpost, and it can
be assumed with confidence that parallels of a higher artistic quality
must have existed in such celebrated synagogues as those of Alexandria
and Antioch. The painting of the Temple above the niche in Dura also
shows the flat roof and the four columns or half-columns, but the doors
are represented as closed, possibly implying a symbolic meaning. A hope of
rebuilding the Temple may have been suggested on the Bar Kochba coins
by the representation of the Ark of the Covenant, whilst in Dura the
closed doors may have implied the loss of the Ark and the abandonment
of faith in an immediate reconstruction of the Temple. Goodenough has
suggested a mystical interpretation for this iconography, but, although a
quest for meaningful explanations is worth attempting, this is not without
difficulty as such symbols frequently elude a rational evaluation.[6] It
should be added at this point that any interpretation that sees in the Dura

*ILL. 11*

painting above the niche a representation of a shrine for the Scrolls, as suggested by Rostovtzeff, is unlikely. The painting is found above the receptacle for the Scrolls and therefore the spectator would be confronted with a meaningless repetition of motifs. The painting of the Temple above the niche at the Synagogue of Dura-Europos expresses the close and growing relationship between Temple and synagogue, the synagogue functioning increasingly as a substitute for the Temple.

Whereas Roman coins depicting Roman temples usually record the temples with pediments, Herod's Temple on the Bar Kochba coins is represented with four columns or half-columns and a flat roof, thereby following the reference in *Middoth*. How far Herod's Temple was inspired by the Solomonic tradition must remain conjectural, but a conscious imitation of the older building, including perhaps the ground plan, seems in keeping with Herod's endeavours to appear as a legitimate and benevolent ruler to his Jewish subjects.[7] At any rate some novel features which distinguish Herod's Temple from the simple prototype of Solomon's Temple, such as the four columns or half-columns, appear to have been incorporated on the coins, and in this manner the earliest extant image of the Temple corresponds with the tradition of the latest building.

*ILL. 12*

Another version of the idealized Temple, the work of a different and probably later hand, is shown on another part, on the third tier, on the western wall of the Dura-Europos synagogue, where it is closely associated with the Tabernacle by a reference to the figure inscribed as Aaron, the first High Priest, signifying the continuity of the priesthood. It is more conventional in form than the painting surmounting the niche, as it is shown as a pedimented façade in the Roman manner. One menorah, as described for the interior of the Tabernacle (*Exodus* 25: 31), is seen in front of the building as an emblem of the Tabernacle in this representation of the Temple. The Temple, according to *Kings* and *Chronicles*, included ten lampstands (I *Kings* 7: 49; II *Chronicles* 4: 7), while *Zachariah* 4: 2 refers to one lampstand only, reminiscent of the menorah of the Tabernacle. The Arch of Titus in Rome, celebrating the destruction of the

*ILL. 2*

Temple, shows, among other trophies, one candlestick only, presumably because there was only one candlestick in Herod's Temple. From the numerous stories connected with the survival of the authentic menorah it can be deduced that the tradition of the menorah is legendary rather than historical.[8]

On the opposite side of the painting of the Aaronic Temple in Dura, seen from the central niche, appears another temple image, showing a pagan place of worship with figures decorating the architecture and fittings, especially the doors. Although these images are as yet not fully explained, they clearly refer to non-Jewish cults, a view not shared by Kraeling. The contrast between the Temple represented as a building symbolizing the tent of the Tabernacle and a pagan place of worship is, therefore, apparent at Dura. This arrangement echoes an old prototype, first found in the so-called Standard of Ur (c. 2500 B.C.), now in the British Museum, which shows the contrast between war and peace. The city of Babylon was represented frequently in mediaeval iconography as the counterpart to the heavenly Jerusalem, especially in Beatus manuscripts, a type which persisted into the fourteenth-century wall paintings of the Palazzo Publico in Siena, vividly expressing the opposition between good and bad government.[9]

The theme of the Dura paintings is based on the Bible with additional Midrashic material. Kraeling's suggestion that there might have been prototypes of biblical images as early as 200 B.C., is based on a belief in the existence of illustrated Greek Bibles of that period intended for the non-Jewish reading public and serving to propagate Jewish culture.[10] It should not be forgotten, however, that the Septuagint was written for Greek-speaking Jews, and such Jews could have been the recipients of illustrated Bibles for home-reading. It is certain, however, that another factor, one emphasizing abstract and symbolic motifs, was also at work, and can be seen, for instance, in the coins of the first and second Revolts which depict emblems of the redemption of Jerusalem. This symbolic approach is still exemplified at Dura in the central panel above the niche representing the Temple with closed doors. There is a similar contrast in Rome between 'pagan' decoration, such as that of the Jewish catacomb of the Vigna Rondanini, incorporating Roman realistic motifs, and abstract, geometric symbolism, such as that of the equally Jewish catacomb of the Via Montana. This contrast is still apparent in comparisons between the German and Spanish schools of Haggadah illustrations, which respectively correspond roughly to a more stylized and a more realistic approach.[11] It is not surprising, therefore, that Hellenized Jews who used the illustrated Septuagint might also have decorated other illuminated manuscripts and painted synagogue walls, of which Dura-Europos is the only known surviving remnant. Here attention should be drawn to the remarkable mosaic found in the Synagogue of Khirbet-Susiiya, showing *ILL. 13* probably the Temple with closed doors flanked by two candlesticks with seven branches. The duplication of the candlesticks is difficult to explain. Mere formal motivation is unconvincing as the sole reason, although the idea of symmetry would commend itself. More important appears a variety of traditions with regard to the material and the shape of the candlestick or candlesticks, which were all mentioned fully in the Babylonian *Talmud*. In addition to these traditions the menorah was interpreted in yet another manner, as a cosmic symbol, by Philo and later writers. It is from such a multiplicity of interpretations of the menorah that the duplication of the form may be explained. This dual arrangement was resuscitated by Nicolaus de Lyra when he contrasted Rashi's and the Church Fathers' designs.[12] The Khirbet-Susiiya mosaic belongs to the fourth or fifth century and is more structural in pattern than the numerous other similar mosaics discovered in Israel, such as those of

*ILL. 14*   Beth-Alpha and Beth She'an. The closed doors and the palmette over the doors are reminiscent of the painting over the niche in Dura. To see here a receptacle for the Scrolls, as sometimes has been suggested, would mean duplication. Such a receptacle was provided in the Torah shrine of the synagogue.[13] It seems astonishing, moreover, that this indulgent attitude to floor decoration was permitted by many rabbis and did not result in more objections at that time.

Another important representation of the Jewish Temple is found on a Roman gilt glass, probably of the fourth century, now in the Vatican

*ILL. 15*   Museum.[14] So far no other example of this type has come to light; the design is of outstanding interest. It shows the Temple, described in Greek as a House of Peace, within a colonnaded court, flanked by the columns Jachin and Boaz, the lampstand with seven branches standing before it. The four columns or half-columns of the façade are represented, but a gabled roof replaces the flat roof. This rare image of the Temple is con-temporaneous with numerous representations of the interiors of synagogues on gilt glass, clearly showing the Shrine for the Scrolls, sometimes with the Scrolls inside it.

So far the pictorial Temple tradition has been considered solely in the context of Judaism. However, this tradition has also left its trace on Christian images of the Temple belonging to this period, especially on the mosaics of the Theotokos Chapel on Mount Nebo, part of a church specifically devoted to the memory of Moses, as Mount Nebo was reputed to be the place of his death, the site from which, according to legend, he viewed the Promised Land. The abstract design of the Temple as repre-sented in the mosaics of the Theotokos Chapel, which can be dated to about A.D. 600, was still based on the façade found on the Bar Kochba coins and repeated above the niche at Dura-Europos. Here the Temple is preceded, however, by a burning fire, and surrounded by a wall, a style reminiscent of the geographical Madaba mosaics as well as of the El-Mehajet mosaics, the latter showing the altar with a flame similar to that represented on Mount Nebo (c. 617–632). [15]

The works here considered show certain specific formal and icono-graphical elements that may suggest characteristic tendencies in Jewish pictorial art. They emphasize symbolic abstraction, evident in the Bar Kochba coins, coupled with historical narrative as seen in the Dura

23

Synagogue decorations, combining both in an artistic synthesis. Moreover, it is obvious that Hellenism played a rôle in the evolution of formal elements, the outstanding protagonist and parallel in philosophy being Philo of Alexandria.[16]

Although the theories of the Jewish philosopher Philo have had no direct bearing on visual art, they do imply a Greek body of opinion not hostile to the arts and favouring allegory and symbolic interpretation. It seems likely that the Greek way of life, including religious imagery, proved generally acceptable to the Jewish communities, as the danger of idol worship had lessened and that, therefore, the Jewish public was ready for pictorial art, including religious subject matter. Only the Torah Scrolls themselves remained unadorned.

It should be remembered that the panel above the niche at Dura shunned realism in favour of abstract representation and, therefore, belongs to an earlier iconographic type. The heritage of Temple imagery was established during the Bar Kochba period, and the theme of the Temple persisted, gaining in importance during the Middle Ages, in the light of Messianic hope in Judaism and a growing realization of the Temple as a 'model' for the church of Christianity.

The iconographic filiation of the ancient Temple picture may be concluded with the famous illumination of the Haggadah of Sarajevo, *ILL. 32* discussed in the second chapter, in which the flat roof shown on the Bar Kochba coins and at Dura was retained, although the perspective became mediaeval. External and internal views were more completely combined, and the Ark of the Law depicted with the Cherubim hiding their heads behind it. In spite of formal differences and adaptations of subject, the ancient prototype based on *Middoth* seems to have remained valid.[17]

### References

1 On the general background see Baron, vols. I and II; cf. G. Vermes's new edition of E. Schuerer, *The History of the Jewish People in the Age of Jesus Christ* (Edinburgh 1973), vol. I, *passim*.

2 S. N. Kramer, *History Begins at Sumer* (2nd edn.: London 1962); A. Parrot, *Sumer* (London and Paris 1961); P. Lampl, *Cities and Planning in the Ancient Near East* (New York 1968).

3 J. Comay, *The Temple of Jerusalem* (London 1975); Baron, vol. II, pp. 280 ff; Hollis, *passim* and pp. 8 ff. On the Tabernacle cf. *Exodus* commentary by J. P. Hyatt in New Century Bible (London 1971). M. Levine, *Le Tabernacle* (Tel Aviv 1968) has to be used with caution.

4 G. F. Hill et al., *A Guide to the Principal Coins of the Greeks* (rev. edn.; London 1959) sect. VIIIA, pl. 49, no. 40 certainly does not represent the screen of the Tabernacle, as suggested. According to the plausible theory of Y. Meshorer, *Jewish Coins of the Second Temple* (Tel Aviv 1967), with excellent bibliography,

a coin reproduced in this study belongs to the third year of the revolt after the loss of Jerusalem, because of its caption 'For the freedom [lecherut] of Jerusalem'. For the pagan parallels to the Temple coins cf. Hill, *op. cit., passim*; the entry 'Coins and Currency' in *Encyclopaedia Judaica*; A. Muehsam, *Coin and Temple* (Leeds 1966); M. Avi-Yonah in J. Neusner, *Religion in Antiquity* (Leiden 1968). The latest contribution to the subject is found in the *British Museum Year Book* (London 1976), vol. I, pp. 39 ff. in a survey by M. Jessop Price.

5   *Palestine Exploration Fund Quarterly Statement*, vol. 68 (1936), p. 158.

6   E. R. Goodenough, *op. cit., passim*, especially vol. IX (Dura) (1964), pp. 69 f. and vol. XII (1965), pp. 160 ff.

7   Cf. W. J. Gross, *Herod the Great* (Baltimore and Dublin 1962); A. Schalit, *König Herodes* (Berlin 1969), pp. 372 ff.

8   L. Ginzberg, *The Legends of the Jews* (Philadelphia 1909–38), *passim*.

9   H. Rosenau, *The Ideal City* (2nd edn.: London 1974), p. 40.

10  C. H. Kraeling et al., *The Excavations at Dura-Europos, Final Report VIII. Part I—The Synagogue* (New Haven 1956), *passim* and pp. 390 ff. See R. Wischnitzer, *The Messianic Theme in the Paintings of the Dura Synagogue* (Chicago 1948); also in *Journal of the American Oriental Society*, vol. 91 (1971), pp. 367 ff.

11  J. Leveen, *The Hebrew Bible in Art* (London 1944), pp. 18 f. Cf. B. Narkiss, *Hebrew Illuminated Manuscripts* (Jerusalem 1969), *passim*. See note 3 of Introduction; V. Mortet, *Recueil de textes relatifs à l'histoire de l'architecture* (Paris 1911), pp. 368 ff.: 'mira quaedam deformis formositas ac formosa deformitas' expresses the views of Bernard of Clairvaux, and is typical of iconoclastic attitudes. See also M. Avi-Yonah, *Ancient Mosaics* (London 1975).

12  See chapter II.

13  M. Avi-Yonah in *Ariel*, vol. 32 (1973), p. 43; E. L. Sukenik, *The Ancient Synagogue of Beth Alpha* (Jerusalem and Oxford 1932). The standard work is still E. L. Sukenik, *Ancient Synagogues in Palestine and Greece* (London 1934).

14  This well-known gilt glass was lately discussed by L. Yarden, *The Tree of Life* (London 1971), p. 29.

15  S. Saller in *Revue Biblique,* vol. XLIII (1934), pp. 120 ff. and P. Lemaire, *ibid.,* pp. 385 ff.

16  On Philo cf. H. A. Wolfson, *Philo. Foundations of Religious Philosophy in Judaism, Christianity and Islam* (Cambridge, Massachusetts 1947), *passim*.

17  This Haggadah is justly famous and the most important book devoted to it is still the first one published: D. H. Müller and J. von Schlosser, *Die Haggadah von Sarajevo* (Vienna 1898). See also C. Roth, *The Sarajevo Haggadah* (London 1963), and M. Metzger, *La Haggada enluminée* (Leiden 1973), vol. I, *passim*, with abundant bibliography. M. Avi-Yonah, *Geschichte der Juden im Zeitalter des Talmud in den Tagen von Rom und Byzanz* (Berlin 1962), especially pp. 188 ff.

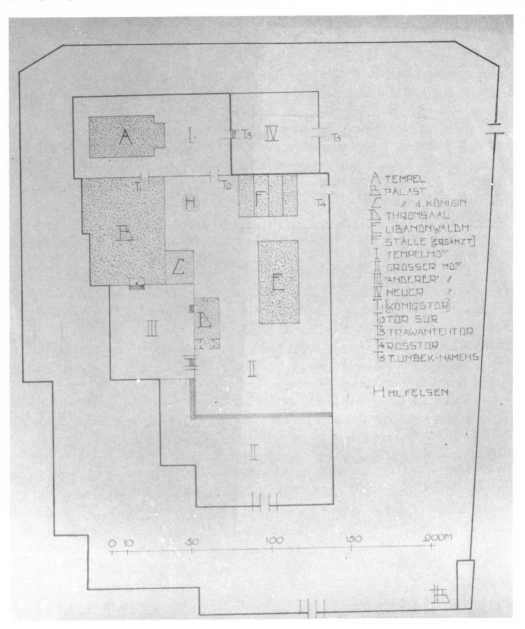

**3** Site plan of Solomon's buildings on Temple Mount, after Busink. 'A' stands for the Temple, 'B' for the palace, 'C' for the palace of the queen, 'D' for the throne chamber, 'E' for the Hall of the Forest of Lebanon, 'F' for the stables, 'I' for the Temple court, 'II' for the large court, 'III' for the 'other court', 'IV' for the 'new court', 'H' for the Holy Rock.

**4** *Gudea* holding a ground plan on his lap
(Paris, Musée du Louvre)

**5** *Gudea,* detail showing ground plan (Paris,
Musée du Louvre)

**6** City of Nippur plan (Jena, University Museum of Jena)

**7** Shekel from Bar Kochba War, obverse showing Temple façade (London, British Museum)

**8** Shekel from Bar Kochba War, reverse showing plant symbols, *lulav* and *etrog* (London, British Museum)

**9** Silver coin, obverse showing head of Claudius (London, British Museum)

**10** Silver coin, reverse showing temple with statue of Diana of Ephesus (London, British Museum)

**11** Synagogue of Dura-Europos, central panel above the niche for the Scrolls (Damascus, Damascus Museum)

**12** Synagogue of Dura-Europos, photomontage of west wall after Kraeling

**15** Roman gilt glass showing the Temple in its Precincts (Rome, Vatican Museum)

(*opposite top*)
**13** Synagogue of Khirbet-Susiiya, mosaic with reconstruction of the Temple (photograph by courtesy of Israel Department of Antiquities and Museums)

(*opposite bottom*)
**14** Synagogue of Beth She'an, mosaic with reconstruction of the Temple (photograph by courtesy of Israel Department of Antiquities and Museums)

**16** Ashburnham Pentateuch, Tabernacle (Paris, Bibliothèque Nationale)

# CHAPTER II

# Abstract Design
# and Structural Vision

THE MIDDLE AGES took over some of the architectural heritage from Antiquity, a heritage largely forgotten during the so-called Dark Ages except in the monasteries, which safeguarded cultural traditions. The ground plan of Sankt Gallen is the most prominent example of such architectural continuity, employing planning techniques used in Antiquity.[1]

The picture of the Temple belongs also to this trend of preservation and is seen in an abbreviated form in certain abstract drawings in which Antique prototypes continued to account for the basic design. An outstanding example is the seventh-century Ashburnham Pentateuch in Paris, written in Latin, which preserves Midrashic material. Its frontispiece shows an arched building within which is a shrine containing the Ten Commandments in Greek letters. This is remarkable in a Latin text and suggests a Judaeo-Greek source. The question whether this illumination represents the Temple or the Tabernacle appears to be difficult to decide at first sight. It can be answered, however, by careful observation, which reveals two columns or half-columns on each side of a building, following in this respect the pattern for the Temple set by the Bar Kochba coins. Furthermore, within the crowning arch, an ornamental form is reminiscent of the design of the palmette in the Temple picture found over the niche in Dura-Europos. For these reasons the building has to be regarded as the Temple, rather than the Tabernacle. On the other hand, fol. 76 shows a sequence of scenes from *Exodus*, including the Tabernacle surrounded by tents and human figures, among them Moses and Joshua. At any rate, the Ashburnham Pentateuch, a Christian biblical manuscript, preserves the Jewish artistic heritage.[2]

More abstract is the depiction of an interior in a Hebrew Pentateuch, dating from the tenth century, now in Leningrad. The lampstand with seven branches and a shrine, probably the Ark of the Covenant, are depicted together with ritual implements. No clearly defined architectural features appear, however, and such an absence suggests that it is the

*ILL. 16*

Tabernacle that is shown.[3] The convergence between the concepts of the Tabernacle and of the Temple can here be observed, demonstrating how the Temple became increasingly a universal symbol, no longer connected with a single site.

The first known literary record of an architectural drawing by a Jew is found in the *Responsa* by Rabbi Solomon ben Isaac (1040–1105) named 'Rashi' from his initials. Rashi was particularly interested in *peshat*, the literary interpretation of sources, and in order to explain an obscure passage about the Temple he wrote to 'the rabbis of Auxerre' on the meaning of verses in *Jeremiah* and in *Ezekiel* (41: 10). 'With regard to what he [Ezekiel] wrote in his question concerning the northern outer chambers, about not being able to understand where they began to the west and how much they extended to the east, and where they began at the inner side and how much they extended outwards—I cannot add anything to what I explained in my commentary, but I will draw a plan [literally 'form' or 'shape'] of them [tsuratam] and send it to him.'[4] The commentary refers, presumably, to *Middoth* IV: 3. These drawings, unfortunately, are lost but the numerous diagrams in later Rashi manuscripts and printed books testify to a strong visual tradition.

Rashi, who was born and died at Troyes, had visited the Rhineland and had studied at Worms. A synagogue existed there in 1034, although nothing of its shape is known. It was replaced in 1174–75 however, and this latter building became one of the most famous Jewish places of worship until its destruction during the Nazi régime. The second synagogue at Worms had two aisles separated by two columns. The column nearer *ILL. 21* to the Ark was adorned by an inscription in Hebrew paraphrasing I *Kings* 7: 15, 16, which describe the erection of the two pillars of Solomon's Temple and this implies a relationship to Hiram of Tyre, the architect of the Solomonic Temple. It is interesting that a parallel exists to Solomon's *ILLS. 18, 19,* Temple in this allusion. The Cathedral of Würzburg has two columns *20* with multiple, as it were oriental-looking, shafts that display the names Jachin and Booz and may belong to the thirteenth century.[5] It is impossible to discover whether the architect or builder of the synagogue at Worms was a Jew for, although the Bishop of Worms befriended the Jews, they could not gain admission to the masons' guilds. There cannot be much doubt, however, that whoever carved the Hebrew script must have been Jewish or influenced by Jews and that, in a subtle way, through the specific inscriptions, Worms synagogue and Würzburg cathedral stood for the Temple. The inclusion of the Worms inscription incidentally refutes Krautheimer's suggestion that a tendency for profanation and secularization characterized the mediaeval synagogue architecture.[6] It must be remembered, of course, that not all synagogues followed the popular

Worms type and that quite a few were composed of undivided halls, usually located on the ground floor but sometimes, probably for safety reasons, placed on the first floor. The niche for the Ark pointed towards Jerusalem and might have been situated on either the long side or the broad side of the buildings concerned.

An interesting set of architectural diagrams accompanies the *Mishnah Commentary* by Maimonides (Moses ben Maimon, called Rambam, 1135–1204), to be seen in the tractate *Middoth*. According to Rabbi D. S. Sassoon these are the work of Maimonides's own hand, but even if this should prove not to be the case the drawings certainly belong to Maimonides's circle. Whilst the main body of the text is in Arabic, it is remarkable that the captions of the drawings are in Hebrew, giving the objects their familiar Jewish names, a linguistic divergence hitherto overlooked.[7]

*ILL. 22*

Maimonides was born in Spain, died in Egypt and was buried at Tiberias. He is the representative of a universal philosophical mind, acquiring fame not only within his own community, in which he remained a respected but controversial figure, but also in the Islamic and Christian worlds.[8] Having been forced to emigrate from his native land, he went to Morocco and Palestine and eventually found a refuge in Egypt, where he was connected with the court of the great Sultan Saladin, acting as court physician. He was known, traditionally, as 'the second Moses' among his supporters, especially because of his *Mishnah Commentary*, including *Middoth*, and his *Mishneh Torah*, an interpretation in fourteen parts of the Jewish code of laws.

The drawings of the *Middoth Commentary* are simple diagrams, not always in proportion but meant as visual aids to the text. They include not only plans of the Temple and its precincts but also many details. Similar in character, but by a more skilled hand, is a ground plan of the Temple, in the Jewish Theological Seminary, New York, accompanying the *Mishneh Torah* of Maimonides, his codification of Jewish law. It shows not only the outline of the Temple, but also the four chambers outside the precincts (*Middoth* I:6) and the Hall of Hewn Stone (*Middoth* V:4) provided with two exedrae at opposite ends,[9] in an ornamental style.

*ILL. 23*

*ILLS. 24, 25*

Another large plan of the Temple exists in two fragments (Kennicott MS 2) at the Bodleian Library, Oxford. According to Thérèse Metzger it is related to the work of Joshuah ben Abraham ben Gaon, who worked in Soria, Old Castile, and was the scribe of MS Paris 20 in the Bibliothèque Nationale, Paris. If this manuscript and other related examples are conclusive, there seems to have existed a flourishing school of illuminators in Soria.[10] The skill of the Jewish map makers, who produced the so-called portolano maps, should also be recalled in this context. Although the surviving maps belong mainly to the fourteenth century, they undoubtedly reflect an older tradition and show the outlines of the continents and the prevalent shipping routes in the form of ground plans. In this way the portolanos are a contrast to the numerous Christian maps of Jerusalem, dating from the twelfth century onwards, which depict detailed elevations of the places of interest to pilgrims.

It was during the twelfth century that the monk Richard of St. Victor (c. 1175) wrote his *In Visionem Ezekielis*, basing his reconstruction of the Temple, unlike Maimonides, on Ezekiel's text. In some aspects Maimonides and Richard of St. Victor appear complementary to each other, especially as the latter's illuminators displayed great skill in elevations. In the English MS Bodley 494 a French prototype can be recognized. It should be *ILLS. 26, 27* stressed at this point that the Jewish manner of depicting the Temple seems to have been based in the mediaeval period largely on the traditional measurements of the ground plan which excluded imaginative reconstructions of the elevations. This represents a striking contrast to the Hellenistic *ILL. 26* and Roman pictorial representations incorporating elevations for Jewish usage, as at that time the image of the Temple was for the Jews a living reality. Richard of St. Victor was particularly interested in the waters (*Ezekiel* 47: 1) issuing from under the Temple towards the east, a motif *ILLS. 26, 27* overlooked in later mediaeval interpretations but revived by Templo during the Baroque period (see chapter V).[11]

Another Jewish type of illumination, gives as it were, an inventory of Temple fittings, outstanding among these being the two Tablets of the Law and the candlestick. It will be remembered, that the former were according to scripture surmounted by two Cherubim, first in the Tabernacle and then in Solomon's Temple (*Exodus* 25: 18, 21; I *Kings* 6: 27; II *Chronicles* 3: 10–13). To the Christian illuminator the Cherubim were popular motifs. But to the Jews, they presented difficulties, because they showed living beings. By contrast, the Tablets of the Law presented no problems, and display little variation in design, whilst the Cherubim show such variations. They stand upright in the Bibles of the Biblioteca Palatina in Parma of 1277 (MS 2268, fol. 7v and 8r) and of the Bibliothèque Nationale, Paris, written in Perpignan in 1299 by Solomon ben Raphael *ILLS. 28, 29* (Hébreu 7, fol. 12v and 13r), whilst they are more realistic, flying in a downward movement, in the manuscript of the Bible of 1301 in the Royal Library in Copenhagen (MS II, fol. 11v and 12r). The Haggadah of *ILLS. 30, 31* Sarajevo, which will be discussed below, illustrates the next stage in abstraction: the heads are hidden. The image of the Cherubim persists in a simplified form even today within the Samaritan community, where they are turned into birds.[12] The last stage of this process, complete elimination of the Cherubim, is seen for instance in the manuscripts

*ILLS. 34, 35,* MS Add. 15250, fol. 3v and 4r and Harley 1528, fol. 7v and 8r of c. 1320,
*36, 37* both in the British Library, and also in the Farhi Bible of 1366–82 (p.
187) in the Sassoon collection. We may assume that the Cherubim were
derived from Christian iconographic sources, and were adapted to
Jewish iconography. However, in Christianity also, as is well known,
opposition to pictures existed. This led to Byzantine and Puritan icono-
clasm, the most outstanding utterance on the subject being perhaps the pun
of St. Bernard of Clairvaux (1090–1153) on 'these beautiful horrors and
these horrible beauties' (see chapter I, note eleven). Jewish illumination
is found in the Haggadoth connected with the festival of Passover, the
Seder service. Among these the Haggadah of Sarajevo, dating from the
middle of the fourteenth century is outstanding. Presumably executed
by Jews, but influenced by Christian prototypes, this Haggadah not only
contains an unusual depiction of the cycle of the Days of Creation,
eliminating the Christian image of God and thus adapting the subject to
Jewish usage, but it also figures an unparalleled image of the Messianic
*ILL. 32* Temple: the centre of the building is occupied by the rectangular Tablets
of the Law, surmounted by two Cherubim with hidden heads. The roof of
the building is flat, like that in the painting above the niche in Dura,
and is adorned by crenellation. Inside and outside views are combined in a
mediaeval artistic convention. Realistic elements were also here introduced
*ILL. 33* and were frequent, showing Jews leaving the synagogue or assembling
at the Seder table; the latter scene was especially popular and is found in
many other manuscripts. But the Days of Creation and the image of the
Temple in architectural form remain unique in the Haggadah of Sarajevo.

The unusual illumination of the Temple there can be explained by the
fusion of two iconographic traditions, one architectural, combining
interior and exterior views and showing a flat roof, the other based on the
representation of ceremonial cult objects. By contrast, the interiors of
synagogues including worshippers are frequently seen in Jewish illuminations, one such in the Haggadah of Sarajevo also combining an interior
and an exterior view. The most outstanding of these is perhaps found in
the manuscript Or. 2884 in the British Library, which abounds in realistic
detail and is paralleled by many interiors which show the reunion of the
family around the Seder table. Thus, the architectural image of the
Temple in the Haggadah of Sarajevo remains unique.

Up to now the focus has been on the biblical tradition in Jewish iconography. In the Christian context, however, it was usual to disregard a
precise reference to scripture and to represent the Temple and the Tabernacle in the contemporary Gothic style. This pattern can be seen in such
works as Petrus Comestor's *Historia Scholastica* written in the late
*ILL. 38* thirteenth century, now in Madrid, which shows symbols of the Temple

in a row of six isolated Gothic structures.[13] Even more marked is the Gothic style in the French *Bible Historiale* by Guyart Desmoulins in the Bodleian Library, Oxford (Douce 211), in which the Tabernacle is represented as a Gothic church and the Ark has the form of a golden reliquary (fols. 67va, 69vb).[14] The iconographic relationship to the Old Testament imagery was here ignored, and the mediaeval world in its new form fully asserted itself. It is in this series of illuminations that perhaps the first ever representation of the candlestick with eight branches, connected with the feast of Chanukkah, appears (fol. 69va). If this is so, the Christian illuminator may well have seen such a candlestick in the house of a Jewish friend.

*ILLS. 39, 40, 41*

*ILL. 41*

The greatest problem in textual interpretation of the Solomonic Temple from an architectural point of view was the disparity between the two texts, that of I *Kings* 6: 2, in which the height of the house is given as twenty cubits, but no height for the porch is mentioned, and that of II *Chronicles* 3: 4, a text also regarded as binding, in which the height of the porch is specified as 120 cubits. In both sources the length of the porch is stated to have been twenty cubits while its breadth, according to I *Kings* 6: 3, amounted to only ten cubits. Such discrepancies already had been noted in the Babylonian *Talmud*. There it is stated that Haninah ben Hezekiah, a sage, tried to resolve still further textual contradictions about the Temple reported in the book of *Ezekiel*, which was regarded by some of his contemporaries as heretical. Haninah tried to reconcile it with the *Torah* and, thus, keep it in the Jewish tradition (*Bab. Menahoth* 45a).[15]

The *Glossa Ordinaria*, a mediaeval commentary on the Bible, suggests that Bede in *De Templo Salomonis Liber* was aware of the contradiction between *Kings* and *Chronicles*,[16] and that he attempted to resolve it by differentiating between the height of the Temple's interior and that of the roof proper without further explanation (*Glossa* II, col. 715; Migne *Patrologiae* etc., vol. 91, col. 749 f.). It is due to Jewish scholars, however, especially Rashi and Kimche, that an attempt was made to harmonize the differences between the measurements in *Kings* and *Chronicles*, whereas the discrepancies raised by Ezekiel, the visionary, were viewed as being of less significance. Maimonides is quite explicit in this respect. The Solomonic Temple as described in *Kings* and *Chronicles* was, by implication, to be as far as possible the model for the Messianic Temple to be built in Jerusalem.[17]

According to Maimonides, the Second Temple, the reconstructed Temple of Zerubbabel, as reported in *Ezra*, followed the Solomonic Temple in the main, although certain suggestions from *Ezekiel* were not ruled out entirely. The Temple of Herod was ignored by Maimonides and the Messianic one can be regarded instead as the Third Temple. This interpretation was adhered to also by Nicolaus de Lyra (1270–1349), a Franciscan monk, who was a famous compiler and interpreter of biblical knowledge, which he laid down especially in his *Postillae*. Outstanding in his work from an architectural point of view is the detailed account of the Jewish Temple, a subject significant for both Jews and Christians. For the Jews the Temple was not only part of past history, but was connected with Messianic hope, for at the advent of the Messiah it would be rebuilt, in the shape recorded for the Solomonic Temple. For this reason the interpretation of the measurements of Solomon's Temple was of practical, although not necessarily immediate, importance as the actual date of the Messiah's appearance is unknown.

For Christians, including Nicolaus de Lyra, there existed not only an historical interest, but even more so a theological concept, the church being regarded as a continuation of, as well as a substitute for, the Temple. In this context, Ezekiel, whose visions were opposed to any specific reconstruction, was viewed as particularly important by Christians.[18] Rabbis and Christian theologians participated in learned discussions and disputations at the very time that witnessed both doctrinal confrontations among Jews and Jewish persecution at the hands of Christians.[19]

A detailed account of Nicolaus de Lyra's interpretation of the Jewish Temple both provides a significant insight into his methods and sheds light on the translation of the textual tradition into visual forms. Nicolaus de Lyra's *Postillae* illustrations were popular during the Middle Ages because they were steeped in the biblical text and gave aesthetic satisfaction. Among the many versions of the illustrations, the two folios in the Bodleian Library, Oxford, are artistically outstanding and seem to reproduce closely the lost original. This fidelity to the original is apparent not only in the Bodleian manuscripts but also from the uniformity found in most such manuscript illustrations and woodcuts and their close affinity to Nicolaus's text.* They support the contention that Nicolaus himself guided and directed the first authentic version of his work.[20]

*ILL. 42* However, in the Nicolaus de Lyra MSS is found the drawing of the elevation of the Solomonic Temple (I *Kings* 6: 2–5), the one design that

---

* My work concentrated on the *Postillae* manuscripts in the Bodleian Library, MSS 251 and Can. Bibl. Lat. 70, and the first illustrated edition by Anton Koberger, *Postillae super Biblia cum additionibus Pauli Burgensis* etc. (Nuremberg 1481). For the Bodleian manuscripts cf. O. Pächt and J. J. G. Alexander, *Illuminated Manuscripts in the Bodleian Library* (Oxford 1966–73), vol. I, nos. 614 and 631. The Koberger edition of 1481 in the British Library (shelf mark I. C.7206) has pencil pagination helpfully added at a later date. These works are quoted here as **Bodley I** and **II** and **Koberger I** and **II** respectively.

does not correspond to the biblical text. A squat building is seen with a high roof and a low 'porticus' and with a *debir* that is rectangular and not a cube, as specified in the Bible, so in this case Nicolaus's text, which adhered to biblical tradition, had not as yet found an appropriate visual form (Bodley I, fol. 150). Perhaps Nicolaus had doubts about this reconstruction, although the low portico and high roof, while departing from the early images of the Temple, find some support in Bede's *De Templo Salomonis Liber* and Rashi's and Kimche's interpretations of the biblical text, discussed below. At any rate the design was regarded as unsatisfactory in the fifteenth century and was replaced in the illustrated *Postillae* edition of 1481 and subsequent editions (Koberger II, fol. F, 176v), which are less in keeping with the Bible than with Nicolaus's manuscript versions. A Gothic tower-like crenellated structure with Gothic windows is shown in its stead, while the pictures of the 'appendicia' and the 'deambulatoria' of the Temple were combined, these having been on separate folios in the manuscript model (Bodley I, fol. 150v and Koberger I, fol. M 218).

*ILL. 43*

Rashi (Rabbi Solomon ben Isaac) suggested in his *Commentary* to *Kings* that the Temple rose in several storeys, drawing on I *Chronicles* 28: 11 as evidence. This passage states that David gave to his son Solomon 'the pattern of the porch and of the houses thereof and . . . of the upper rooms thereof'. Rashi used this quotation to emphasize that there were indeed such upper storeys.[21] David Kimche (1160–1235) went even further in stressing that all the parts of the Temple buildings are mentioned separately. This implies that the upper storeys belonged to the porticus only, thus giving the effect of a tower, a visual conclusion not reached by Kimche but left to Nicolaus de Lyra, who visualized the concept in his text, where he suggested that the Temple was a large building and had a square tower with a flat roof ('facta ad modum turris quadrate', following *Genesis* 35: 6 in the Vulgate), 'according to the manner of houses in Palestine' ('modum domorum palestine') (Bodley I, fol. 150, col. a; Koberger I, fol. M 219, col. a).[22]

Nicolaus is imprecise in his description, but it is in dealing with the *Ezekiel* illustration of Nicolaus's *Postillae* that the theory of the square tower comes to the fore, and this is in two different parts of the Temple Precincts, the first for the eastern gate of the eastern porch of the Temple, the second for the Temple porticus proper. Both illustrations show symmetrical side turrets but of different shapes, the former being round and set on corbels, the latter square and rising from the ground.

*ILL. 44*

The elevation of the entrance to the Temple precincts is given as twenty-five cubits, a figure connected with detailed calculations and especially *Ezekiel* 40: 13, 21, in which the breadth of the building is given that size.

A closed doorway on the ground floor is perhaps suggested by *Ezekiel* 44: 1, and Nicolaus assumed a height of forty cubits for the elevation of the porticus, following a tradition based on *Middoth* III: 7 and IV: 6 in which the measurements of the entrance to the Temple are recorded as forty cubits high and twenty cubits wide. As Nicolaus's text does not mention a source, he was presumably dependent on oral communication. Nicolaus de Lyra also included the slanting windows ('fenestras obliquas') of I *Kings* 6: 4 and *Ezekiel* 40: 16 in order to illustrate his text (Bodley II, fol. 154v, col. a and 158v).

The Solomonic Temple, according to the Bible, was surrounded by three rows of chambers, the appendicia, and these were variously interpreted by biblical commentators. The entrance was on the right-hand corner and was usually reconstructed as a spiral staircase (I *Kings* 6: 8; *Ezekiel* 41: 6–7; *Middoth* IV: 5), reproduced also on the left-hand corner by Nicolaus de Lyra for reasons of safety against fire but, presumably, also because of aesthetic considerations (Bodley II, fol. 158v; Koberger II, fol. F 176v).

Most of the illuminations of Nicolaus de Lyra's text provided the models for later versions of the *Postillae* and were also used in Hartmann Schedel's *Liber Cronicarum* of 1493.[23] For the tower motif as such Nicolaus mentions *Genesis* 35: 21, which in the Vulgate speaks of 'fixit Tabernaculum trans turrem gregis' (Bodley I, fol. 150, col. a; Koberger I, fol. M 219, col. a). The woodcuts of Koberger and subsequent editions of the *Postillae* follow the prototype of the manuscripts, adding text and ground plans for clarification and incorporating Gothic features. As was usual, the manuscript that formed the basis of the Koberger illustrated edition seems to have been destroyed whilst the woodcuts were done from it.

In the picture of the eastern porch of the atrium of the Temple the measurements of the doorway have been omitted or forgotten in Bodley II
*ILL. 45* (fol. 154 a) but the porch as well as the portico elevations features the eastern doorway in a prominent manner in Koberger's edition (Koberger II, fols. F 174, F 176v). Nicolaus interprets the 'winding passage' ('mesibbah') of the Temple as twin towers, each with a spiral staircase ('coclea'), giving access to the appendicia (I *Kings* 6: 5; *Middoth* IV: 5; *Ezekiel* 41: 6, 7). The side chambers of the Temple are designed as separate
*ILL. 46* towers on a square base in Nicolaus de Lyra's manuscripts (Bodley II, fol. 158v), while the tower-like façade with twin turrets and slanting
*ILL. 47* windows is based in both Bodley II and Koberger on the measurements recorded in II *Chronicles* 3: 4. The structure culminates, also in both representations, in a crenellated roof, which appears also in the view of the
*ILL. 32* Temple in the Sarajevo Haggadah. The two symmetrical flanking towers are meant to represent the cells that, according to tradition, surrounded

41

the Temple on three sides. It should be noted that the singular artistic effect is related neither to the contemporary evocations of a church nor to those of a secular building.

In specifying the elevations based on *Ezekiel*, precision was impossible in view of the obscurity of the text and the fact that it seems originally to be based on a ground plan, without any precise knowledge of elevations. In the circumstances, Nicolaus de Lyra was able to give a convincing image of an overpowering building which, while within the style of his period, created a form *sui generis* and was not reminiscent of a church. His scheme was resuscitated later in the elevation of the tower of the Temple in the Renaissance style reconstructed by Benedictus Arias Montanus, who seems to have reached this conclusion independently as *ILL. 91* he does not mention Nicolaus de Lyra.

The ground plan of the Temple in its most complete form is found in the diagram by Maimonides in his *Commentary* to *Middoth*. This type *ILL. 22* may have influenced Nicolaus de Lyra, for not only are the main outlines and proportions similar but, in the Oxford manuscript (Bodley II, fol. *ILL. 48* 165v), the ramp for the Altar of the Holocaust is incorporated in symmetrical form, following *Exodus* 20: 26, *Middoth* III: 7 and Josephus's *Jewish War*. Nicolaus de Lyra was probably advised by Jews who are not singled out by name, for obvious reasons: he did not wish to be regarded as a Judaizer. In other illuminations of the same manuscript, and in the printed editions, this detail of the ramp is omitted, which assures *ILL. 49* for Bodley II a special place in the pictorial tradition of the Temple.

Even more revealing of the relationship between Jews and Christians is the type of ground plan showing the encampments of the Jewish tribes round the sanctuary, as suggested in the manuscripts of Rashi, Maimonides and Nicolaus de Lyra (Bodley II, fol. 163; Koberger II, fol. G, 180v). The main outlines are identical in all three sources, and even the differences are insignificant.

Although forming part of the Temple Precincts rather than the Temple itself, the Hall of the Forest of Lebanon should also be mentioned (I *ILL. 50 Kings* 7: 2–4). As it appears in Koberger, this shows an early type of *ILL. 51* High Gothic tracery, with crenellation and the division of the hall into four aisles, thus following an incorrect interpretation of the Vulgate, the original text stating that there were four rows of columns in the hall, which would imply a building of five aisles (Bodley I, fol. 151v; Koberger I, fol. M 218v).

When studying Nicolaus de Lyra's text, especially his inclusion of numerous explanatory French words and some Hebrew words in isolation, one cannot but agree with the view of his hostile commentator, Paul of Burgos or Paul de Santa Maria, the former Jew Solomon ha Levi (1354–

1435), that Nicolaus concentrated too much on the literal sense, on Rashi and that his Hebrew was deficient (Koberger I, fols. 16ff.). Nicolaus was, however, primarily an educator, and for this reason he interspersed his text with French words in order to clarify the Latin text, e.g., the expression 'viz' for 'coclea', in order to explain the winding passage as two spiral staircases (Bodley II, fols. 154, col. b, 154v, col. a; Koberger II, fol. F 174) or 'archieres' as an explanation of the 'fenestras obliquas', loopholes for shooting arrows.

As mentioned above, Jewish informants influenced the work of Nicolaus de Lyra, but seem not to have been converts, as has been suggested.[24] Their approach was of a positive nature, for which reason Nicolaus sometimes contradicts them, and it would be unreasonable to expect Nicolaus to have identified his living Jewish contacts more closely.[25] Not only was exact citation of sources unusual at the time, but also such citations could hardly have proven beneficial to them. Furthermore, these revelations of sources easily might have led to charges of Judaizing, particularly in a period in which the Franciscan Order was rent by conflicts between the Conventuals and the Spirituals. As a Franciscan, Nicolaus had to be circumspect at a time when his Order was in open feud with the Dominicans.[26]

It is clear therefore that, although not a visionary and not an erudite Hebrew scholar, Nicolaus de Lyra nevertheless displayed great ingenuity in making the mysterious visible and easily understood. In this sense he was a great educator, sharing with Rashi and Maimonides a deep interest in the Jewish tradition, although Maimonides's primary concern was the rebuilding of the Solomonic Temple with all its ritual as exactly as possible, in preparation for the arrival of the Messiah. In spite of his interest in Jewish matters Nicolaus de Lyra remained in the mainstream of the Christian tradition. Ezekiel's vision, simply because of its imaginative character, was regarded as foreshadowing the church, not to be understood as some material structure but as a spiritual Temple.[27]

## References

1 On Sankt Gallen cf. K. J. Conant, *Carolingian and Romanesque Architecture* (Harmondsworth 1959; rev. edn.: 1973), pp. 19 ff.

2 J. Sauer, *Symbolik des Kirchengebäudes* (Freiburg 1902) is still relevant on the background; O. von Gebhardt, *The Miniatures of the Ashburnham Pentateuch* (London 1883); B. Narkiss in *Cahiers Archéologiques*, vol. XIX (1969), pp. 45 ff. and vol. XXII (1972), pp. 19 ff.; W. Neuss, *Die Katalanische Bibelillustration* etc. (Leipzig and Bonn 1922); J. Gutmann in *Jewish Quarterly Review*, n.s. vol. 44 (1953), pp. 55 ff.; J. Gutmann (ed.), *The Temple of Solomon* (Missoula 1976); J. Gutmann (ed.), *No Graven Images, passim.*

3 B. Narkiss, *Hebrew Illuminated Manuscripts* (Jerusalem 1969), pl. 1, p. 42. It is most unlikely that the two isolated pillars in the Leningrad Pentateuch, unequal in height, should be meant to show Jachin and Boaz, as tentatively suggested by Narkiss.

4 H. Hailperin, *Rashi and the Christian Scholars* (Pittsburgh 1963). The translation is based on the one kindly provided by Mr. R. A. May; it differs from Hailperin on p. 283. Mr. May's translation is based on I. Elfenbein's edition of Rashi's *Responsa* (New York 1943), pp. 1 and 4 f. B. Smalley, *The Study of the Bible in the Middle Ages* (2nd edn.: Oxford 1952).

5 O. Böcher, 'Die Alte Synagogue zu Worms', *Der Wormsgau,* supplement 18 (1960). W. Cahn in *The Temple of Solomon, op. cit.,* pp. 45 ff.

6 R. Krautheimer, *Mittelalterliche Synagogen* (Berlin 1927). On halls with two aisles see E. Le Nail, *Le Château de Blois* (Paris 1875), still useful for text and illustrations. For a first-class study of the double-aisled hall in England cf. M. Wood, *The English Mediaeval House* (London 1965), *passim.*

7 On Maimonides's drawings cf. J. Fromer, *Maimonides Commentar zum Tractat Middoth* (Breslau 1898) and the facsimile published by D. S. Sassoon, *Maimonidis Commentarius in Mischnam* (Copenhagen 1966), especially vol. III.

8 The article by R. Wischnitzer in *Journal of Jewish Art*, vol. I (1974), pp. 16 ff. misinterprets the drawings historically by assessing them as if they were technical works, cf. H. Rosenau on Nicolaus de Lyra and the Jewish tradition in *Journal of Jewish Studies*, vol. XXV (1974), pp. 294 ff. See also B. Narkiss in *Journal of Jewish Art, op. cit.,* pp. 6 ff.

9 On this tradition see A. Büchler, *Das Synedrion in Jerusalem* etc. (Vienna 1902).

10 Thérèse Metzger in *Bulletin of the John Rylands Library* (offprint), vol. 52 (1970), pp. 1 ff. and vol. 53 (1970), pp. 41 ff., especially p. 17 in vol. 52, with excellent bibliography. L. Bagrow and R. A. Skelton, *History of Cartography* (London 1964) pp. 61 ff.

11 O. Pächt and J. J. G. Alexander, *Illuminated Manuscripts in the Bodleian Library* (Oxford 1966–73), vol. III, no. 185, MS Bodley 494; J. P. Migne, *Patrologiae Cursus Completus*, vol. 196, cols. 527 ff.

12 Information and photograph kindly supplied by Mr. R. D. Barnett.

13 C. O. Nordström, 'The Temple Miniatures in the Peter Comestor Manuscript at Madrid', *Horae Soederblomianae*, vol. VI (1964), pp. 54 ff. Also Nordström's 'The Duke of Alba's Castilian Bible', *Figura*, n.s. vol. 5 (1967).

14 H. Rosenau in *Cahiers Archéologiques*, vol. XIII (1962), pp. 39 ff. A less usual type of interior in Temple illuminations is published by R. Hausherr in *Frühmittelalterliche Studien*, vol. VI (1972), pp. 356 ff. Pächt and Alexander, *op. cit.,* vol. I, no. 581.

15 Babylonian *Talmud*, trans. E. Cashdan (London 1948), p. 272.

16 *Biblia Sacra cum Glossa Ordinaria* (Antwerp 1617), cited here as *Glossa.*

17 Maimonides, *The Book of Temple Service, Code,* trans. M. Lewittes (New Haven 1957), vol. VIII, sect. I. 4, p. 5. Also *Palestine Exploration Fund Quarterly Statement* (1885), pp. 30 f. See also note 7.

18 W. Zimmerli, *Ezechiel, Biblischer Kommentar zum Alten Testament* (Neukirchen 1955); W. Neuss, *Das Buch Ezechiel in Theologie und Kunst* etc. (Münster 1912). Migne, *Patrologiae.*

19 W. P. Eckert in *Monumenta Judaica, 2000 Jahre Geschichte und Kultur der Juden am Rhein, Handbuch* (Cologne 1963), pp. 141 ff.

20  H. Rosenau in *Journal of Jewish Studies*, vol. XXV (1974), pp. 294 ff.

21  *Biblia Rabbinica* (Amsterdam 1727), vol. IV, fol. 396v. Translation kindly contributed by Mr. E. Silver.

22  I am indebted to M. François Avril for a survey of the Nicolaus de Lyra manuscripts in the Bibliothèque Nationale, Paris. Cf. P. Lauer, *Catalogue général des manuscripts latins, Bibliothèque Nationale, Paris* (Paris 1939 etc.). The *Postilla*, in John Rylands Library, finished in 1402 and of Italian origin, has also been consulted. Cf. M. R. James, *A Descriptive Catalogue of the Latin Manuscripts in the John Rylands Library* (Manchester 1921), nos. 29–31, as well as the Strasbourg printed edition of 1492.

23  F. J. Stadler, *Michael Wolgemut und der Nürnberger Holzschnitt* (Strasbourg 1913).

24  Hailperin, *op. cit.*, pp. 290–91.

25  This fact discredits the unsupported suggestion by C. H. Krinsky in *Journal of the Warburg and Courtauld Institutes*, vol. 33 (1970), pp. 1 ff., that Nicolaus was of Jewish extraction.

26  D. L. Douie, *Archbishop Pecham* (Oxford 1952), *passim*.

27  Bodley II, fol. 169, col. a; Koberger II, fol. H 185v, col. b. On the general problem cf. Y. M. J. Congar, *The Mystery of the Temple* etc. (London 1962).

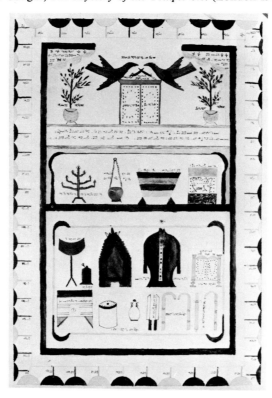

**17**  Watercolour sketch by a Samaritan Bar Mitzvah boy (courtesy of Dr. R. D. Barnett)

18   Cathedral of Würzburg, two mediaeval columns (Würzburg, Bischöfliches Bauamt)

**19, 20**   Cathedral of Würzburg, capitals of two mediaeval columns (Würzburg, Bischöfliches Bauamt)

21  Worms Synagogue, before Nazi destruction, capitals of columns (from an old photograph)

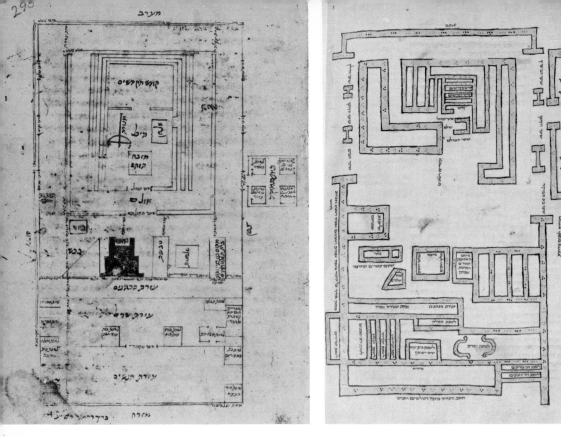

(*above left*)
**22**  Maimonides, *Mishnah Commentary,* ground plan of Temple (Oxford, Bodleian Library)

(*above right*)
**23**  Maimonides, *Mishneh Torah,* ground plan of Temple Precincts (New York, Jewish Theological Seminary)

**24, 25** Fragments of plan of Temple Precincts
(Oxford, Bodleian Library, Kennicott 2)

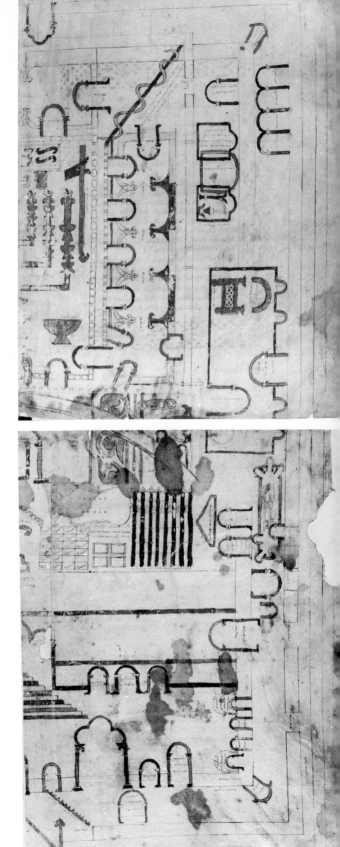

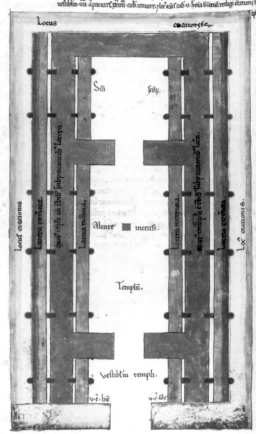

(*above left*)
**26** Richard of St. Victor, *In Visionem Ezekielis,* Temple elevation (Oxford, Bodleian Library, Bodley 494, 156r)

(*above right*)
**27** Richard of St. Victor, *In Visionem Ezekielis,* ground plan of Temple (Oxford, Bodleian Library, Bodley 494, 158v)

(*opposite top, left*)
**28** Paris Pentateuch, Temple fittings (Paris, Bibliothèque Nationale, Hébreu 7, 12v)

(*opposite top, right*)
**29** Paris Pentateuch, Temple fittings (Paris, Bibliothèque Nationale, Hébreu 7, 13r)

(*opposite bottom, left*)
**30** Copenhagen Pentateuch, Temple fittings (Copenhagen, Royal Library, Hebr. 2, 11r)

(*opposite bottom, right*)
**31** Copenhagen Pentateuch, Temple fittings (Copenhagen, Royal Library, Hebr. 2, 12v)

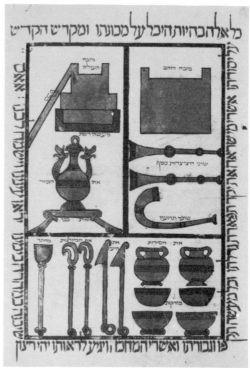

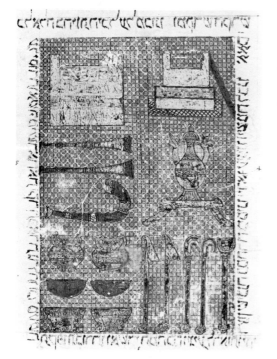

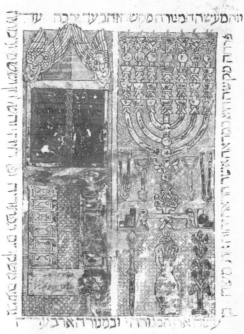

(*above left*)
**32**  Haggadah of Sarajevo, 'Messianic Temple' (Sarajevo, Museum)

(*above right*)
**33**  Haggadah of Sarajevo, synagogue (Sarajevo, Museum)

(*opposite top, left*)
**34**  Temple fittings (London, British Library, Add. 15250, 4a)

(*opposite top, right*)
**35**  Temple fittings (London, British Library, Add. 15250, 3b)

(*opposite bottom, left*)
**36**  Temple fittings (London, British Library, Harley 1528, 7v)

(*opposite bottom, right*)
**37**  Temple fittings (London, British Library, Harley 1528, 8r)

 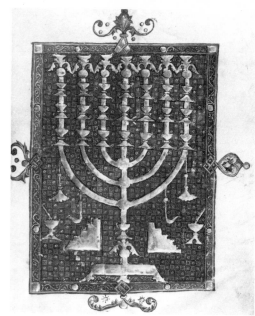

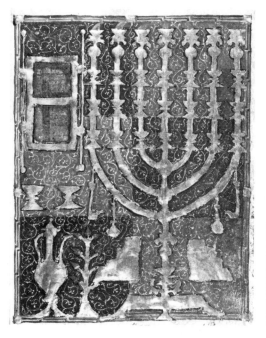 

**38** Petrus Comestor, *Historia Scholastica,* Temple interior (Madrid, Biblioteca Nacional, Codex Reservado 1299, 6v and 7r)

**39** Guyart Desmoulins, *Bible Historiale,* Tabernacle (Oxford, Bodleian Library, Douce 211)

**40** Guyart Desmoulins, *Bible Historiale,* Cherubim above Mercy Seat (Oxford, Bodleian Library, Douce 211)

**41** Guyart Desmoulins, *Bible Historiale,* candlestick with eight branches (Oxford, Bodleian Library, Douce 211)

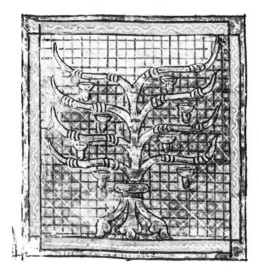

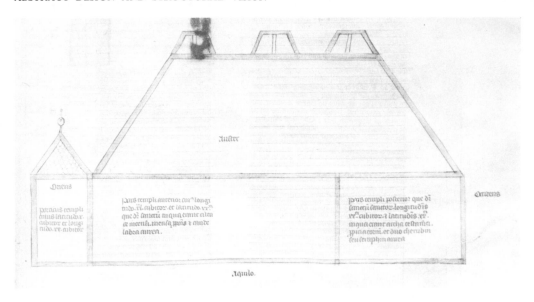

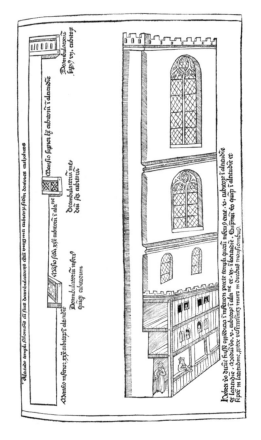

(*above*)
**42** Nicolaus de Lyra, *Postillae,* Temple elevation (Oxford, Bodleian Library)

(*left*)
**43** Koberger *Postillae,* Temple elevation (London, British Library)

(*opposite*)
**44** Nicolaus de Lyra, *Postillae,* entrance to Temple Precincts (Oxford, Bodleian Library)

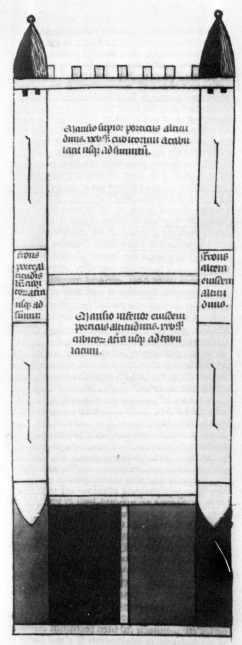

Mansio supior porticus altitudinis xxv.p. cubitorum ab tabulatu usque ad summum.

frons porte altitudinis eiusdem cum ea corona usque ad summum.

frons altera eiusdem altitudinis.

Mansio inferior eiusdem porticus altitudinis xxv.p. cubitorum alia usque ad tabulatum.

Hic supius est in figura aspectus altitudinis porte orientalis atque erectois uenientis ad ipam aporta in muro erctionis et idem est intelligendum de aliis eiusquis porte. nam in b sunt omnino. in primo ad exponem tur teutamur. et uenit ad portam que respiciebat uiam orientalem. b est porta bi muri ad quam uenit de porta orientali in primo muro bi erctionis. et ascendit p gradus eius. et. e. cub pat quod gradus uti erant cur portam muro uulgi. qa prius ascendit derus gdus. et postea occurrit sibi limen porte mensuradum .si. u. eent isti gradus intra portam ut

diat magi nardus de sco victore ut inspiciut iuue muru porte ut dicant aliqui applia diuersit mensuris est limen porte. et ascendit p gradus eius iuue prius occurrit mensurati qui gradus ascensus. et mensus est limen porte calamo uno latitudinem. bm mum medy spiritudinem. ei in ybreo sic hetur. et mensus est poste porte. et di portis otiu pe num ascendens sursum bu alatitudinem ethi er una pte cuius latitudo et bm spiritudinem uium. sicut et limus. Wel limen uiui. b nidetur tra corrupta p lectores ponentes .i. pro. et. nam in ybeo sic hetur. et pote uium. x. et nam ostum q̈ b dicitur porta ht duos potes. l. dextrum et sinistrum et equalis meusure et simili duplr lime. l. inferius et sup pius. et eiusdem meusure p quod no uariatur meusura si dicatur lime bm tusionem in au ut poste bm hebos et thalamu .i. anentn. bi. tha lamorum. ex breuiter accipi singulare p plurii. uno calamo inlongum. et uno calamo inlatum. istud spacium quadratum est intelligendum te pretes thalamorum. itã p mum claudentes i dinudentes thalacuos sunt er mesuram istam io subditur. et mensurauit thalamos .v. cubitos dicit ue comune expositores qui quia minorum di deucuum ut thalamos hebat quinque cubitos inspiraltidine cuius meusurat porte hic. nam spiritudo mum dinudentis mur thalamu. si no est biliunte qi spiritudo mum dinudentis esset tanta cum spacium cuius thalami. sic enim sex cubitorum in quadra ut dictum est. et io meutus vi q̈ p ij q̈ di inc. et mensurauit thalamos quin q̈ cubitos. intelligantur duo muru dinudentes tres thalamos er una pte. et spiritudo cuius idbz. sit duorum cubitorum et dinudi i ide est mesurudum est inicibus thalamu er pate altera. et limen porte. sic hetur. in hebreo er quo pe q̈ sup no meusurautur duo limina qi est sut. li meusurautur .i. porte ut dictum est. b qi limina. et accipi li singulare p plurii. nam me surato uno limine hetur meusura altitus. quia sunt eiusdem meusure ut porteum est. iurta uestibulum porte inteusecus. in hebreo hetur. iuri porticum porte inteusecus. qi porticus est intra portam inuatuo erctiois. uel diuidu a. er in loco uulgi ut sup dictum est. calamo uno. b est mensura limnis cuius latitudo est bm spili audine murum quin medy. et mensus est uestibuli porte. hebus sic hi. et mensus est porticum porte otto cubitorum. tm eum occupabat de atrio er ciois ut porteam procedendo ab oriente incedat teui. et exporteui eius duobus cubitis. defrontibus porte dicat. Ita fa. q̈ sunt pillaru rotundi adhe tes mum medio apte erciois. vnus ad dextram porte. et alius ad sinistram. eleuati sursum ut totum porte edifitiu i spiritudo cuius. siue diamet est duor cubitorum. et sic exponit q̈ di hi. et fronteu eius .i. q̈ r duarum frouau duobus cubitis. l. i spiritudine. li h no uidetur bm. nam me i. q̈ infrontibus erant eauelse obtique ad dandum lume maius. q̈ uo est uisi uterii frouteus eent couunentes aliq̈ inqua saltei tieru ascensus sursum p eodeui que galt di uit. b aue de no pot ut arauium cuius dya met est duorum cubitorum eu. et io meutus dicitur qi froutes iste sunt due tuuele er utrq̈ pte porte ut poteum est tante latitudiuis

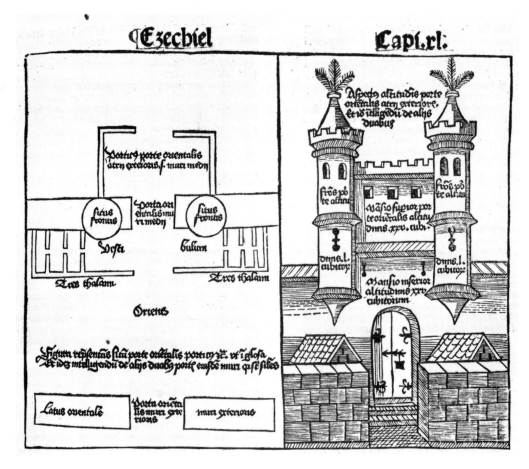

45 Koberger *Postillae,* entrance to Temple Precincts (London, British Library)

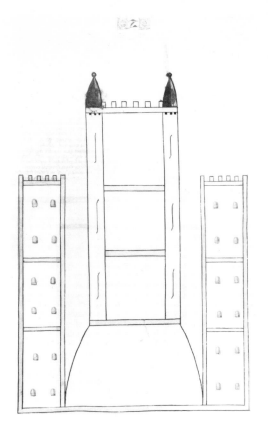

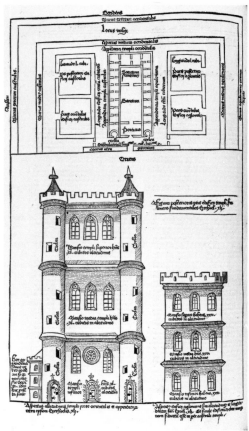

(*above left*)
**46**   Nicolaus de Lyra, *Postillae,* Temple elevation (Oxford, Bodleian Library)

(*above right*)
**47**   Koberger *Postillae,* ground plan and Temple elevations (London, British Library)

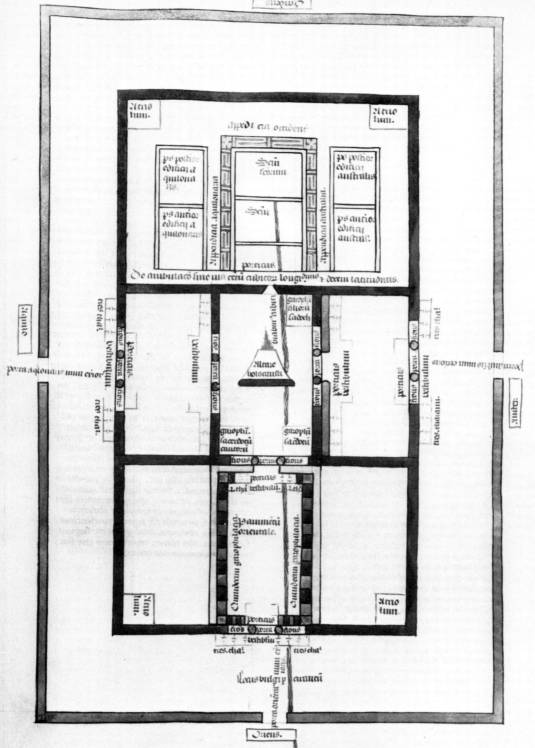

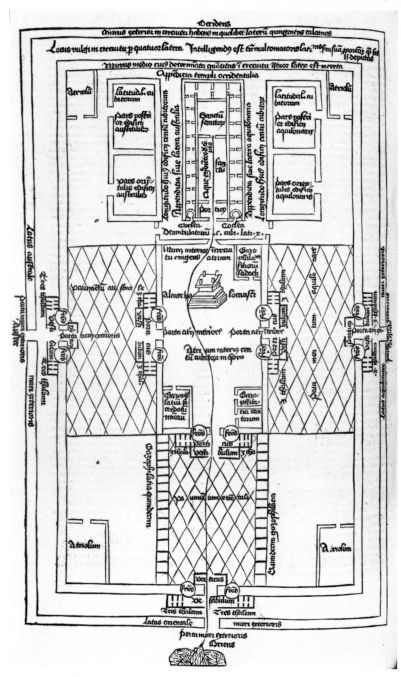

(*opposite*)
**48** Nicolaus de Lyra, *Postillae,* ground plan of Temple Precincts (Oxford, Bodleian Library)
(*above*)
**49** Koberger *Postillae,* ground plan of Temple Precincts (London, British Library)

61

Frons domus saltus libani.

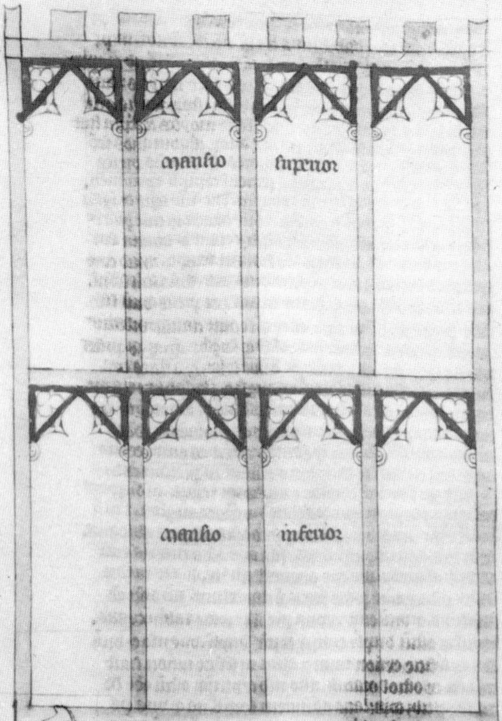


Domum autem. Hic vii. agitur de edificiis domorum regalium, et primo ca-dechius modi edificiis agitur. Secundo ad ornamentum aliquorum viridentibus domus domini nobilia vasa, ibi. Fecit quoque rex. ¶ Circa primum sciendum quod secundum doctores nostros Salomon fecit tria edificia. Unum pro habitatione sua. Aliud pro habitatione uxoris sue, scilicet filie Pharaonis. Et tertium quod vocabatur domus saltus libani, eo quod circa illud edificium erant viridaria arboribus consita. De primis duobus edificiis parum loquitur scriptura, et hoc forte quia erant de consimili opere sicut et domus saltus libani que hic describitur satis diffuse ut videbitur, hoc tamen excepto quod in domo saltus libani erant due mansiones, una inferior et alia superior. Superior in palatio regis parabatur, in habitatione inferiori servabantur unguenta et pigmenta et aromata et huiusmodi, propter quod parietes erant de lapidibus et talia possent ibi melius servari. In superiori vero ponebatur armamentarium et erat tota de lignis in parietibus et columpnis, et in utraque mansione erant tres ordines columpnarum, et in quolibet ordine erant xv. columpne, id est xlv. in universo. Et erant isti ordines secundum longitudinem domus, ita quod erant ibi quatuor deambulatoria. Duo inter columpnas et unum inter columpnas et parietem in uno latere, et aliud inter columpnas et parietem in alio latere per modum autem predictum, prout hic est capitulo figuratum quantum ad frontem domus. Pavimentum autem eius figuratur in pagina sequenti. Et tectum erat planum, quia sic fiebant in terra illa, et in circuitu muri erant propugnacula per que tuebantur stillicidia, proicientia extra aquam pluvialem. Super deambulatoria superiora erant trabes arcuales laqueati tabulis cedrinis. Et fuit hoc expressum cum dicitur: domum suam fecit Salomon xiii. annis. Et loquitur de istis tribus edificiis que omnia erant Salomonis quamvis essent diversis usibus applicata, ut dictum est. Et propter hoc maius tempus apposuit Salomon in edificatione domus domini. ¶ Item quia pro edificatione domus domini erant multe expense parate per regem David, ut patet primo paralipomenon. ¶ Item quia ipse erat magis devotus et intentus ad edificationem domus domini. Consequenter describit in speciali domum saltus libani in longitudine, latitudine et altitudine, et patet litera ex dictis, hoc excepto quod altitudo hic accipitur secundum aliquos usque ad mansionem superiorem tantum, secundum alios vero usque ad tectum domus. Et super columpnas quadrangulata ligna ad portandum tecta. Consequenter describit porticus existentes ante domum pro habitatione regia, cum dicitur: Et porticum columpnarum fecit quinquaginta cubitorum longitudinis, id est secundum mensuram latitudinis domus, et ex hoc patet quod ista domus erat talis in latitudine domum saltus libani. Ante vero porticum istam magnam erant due alie porticus minores, una iuxta aliam in longitudine maioris porticus, et in una tenebantur iudicia communia. In alia vero erat thronus Salomonis in quo sedebat quando volebat esse in iudiciis, et hoc est quod dicitur: Alteram porticum in facie maioris porticus. Hec est illa porticus in qua erant iudicia communia. Et columpnas quibus claudebatur porticus. Et epistilia, id est capitella que erant super columpnas ad decorem. Et domuncula, id est thronus Salomonis mirabili opere factus, ut habetur infra x. ca. ¶ Consequenter descendit scriptura ad describendum domum regine cum dicitur: Domum quoque fecit etc. tali opere quali et hanc porticum. Non quantum ad hoc quod clauderetur columpnis, sed quia parietes erant de consimili materia cum muro qui erat sub columpnis porticus, quia columpne ille claudentes porticum non descendebant usque ad terram, sed erant posite super murum habentem aliquam altitudinem, licet non magnam, et hoc est quod dicitur: Omnia lapidibus preciosis et cetera. Hebrei dicunt ponderosis. Usque ad atrium maius. Istud atrium non erat atrium domus domini, sed domus regie, propterea subditur postea: Et atrium maius rotundum. Atrium enim domus domini quadratum erat ut dictum est capitulo precedenti.

Descriptio pavimenti domus saltus libani.

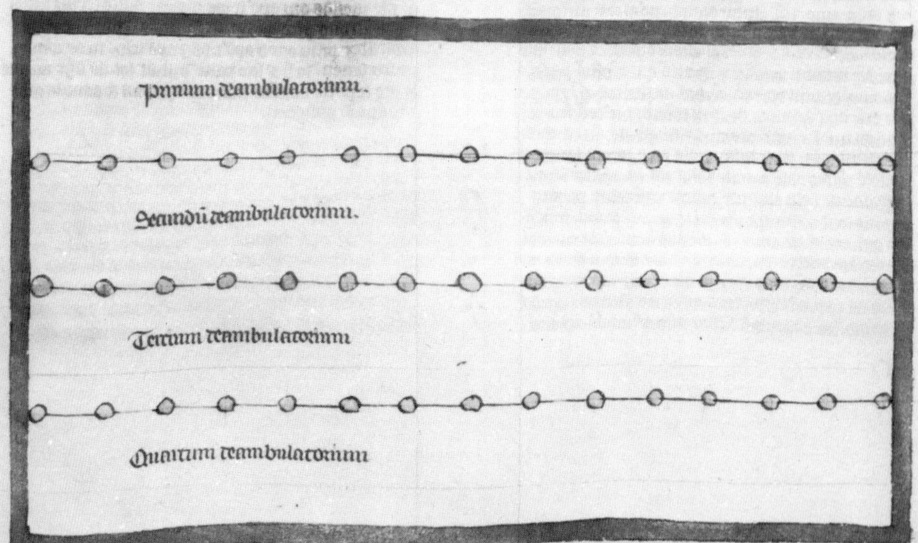

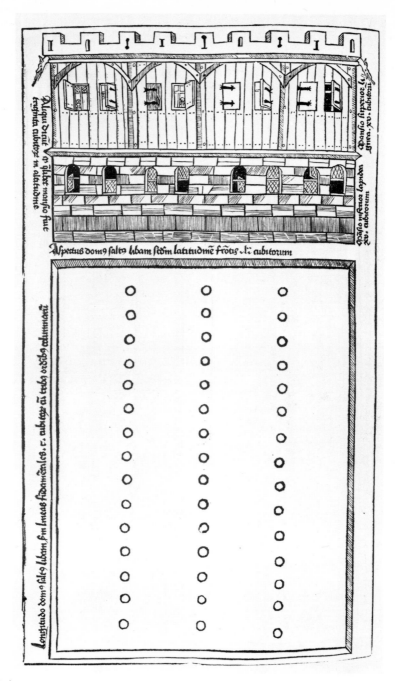

(*opposite*)
**50**   Nicolaus de Lyra, *Postillae,* Hall of the Forest of Lebanon (Oxford, Bodleian Library)
(*above*)
**51**   Koberger *Postillae,* Hall of the Forest of Lebanon (London, British Library)

**52** Hubert van Eyck (attributed to), *The Three Marys at the Open Sepulchre,* with a view of Jerusalem, including the Dome of the Rock (Rotterdam, Boymans-van Beuningen Museum)

# CHAPTER III

# Aspects of Realism

IT WAS A moment of great significance when the octagonal mosque in Jerusalem, best known as the Dome of the Rock, became the church of the Knights Templars, after 1119.[1] On the top of the cupola they affixed

*ILL. 53*   their emblem, the cross, and in this manner the form of the original mosque influenced the design not only of the Templars' churches, but also those based on the Holy Sepulchre in Jerusalem with the same central layout. These established a prototype that was adopted all over Europe.[2] The structure of the Templars' church was represented on their seals, such as the characteristic one of Father Andreas de Coloors, Preceptor of the

*ILL. 54*   Houses of Templars in France ('Domorum Templi Francia Preceptor'), dating from 1214, an early date for such realistic rendering. When the Templars occupied the holy site they first took over the al-Aksa mosque as part of the Temple Precincts and called it the 'Palatium' or 'Templum Salomonis'.[3]

The octagonal church on the Temple site fascinated later mediaeval illuminators as is seen, for instance, from its inclusion in the background of a painting generally attributed to Hubert van Eyck, now in the Boymans-

*ILL. 52*   van Beuningen Museum, Rotterdam.[4] The shape is found not only in Jewish illuminated manuscripts and wall paintings[5] but also in Bernhard von Breydenbach's *Peregrinatio in Terram Sanctam*, published in 1486, of which numerous editions and translations exist. The plates are the work of Erhard Reuwich.[6]

*ILL. 60*   In Breydenbach's *Peregrinatio* the Dome of the Rock is seen on a folding plate, showing a general view of Jerusalem. This type also influenced one of the plates (fols. LXIIIv, LXIVr) of Hartmann Schedel's *Liber*

*ILLS. 55, 56*   *Cronicarum* of 1493. It shows the Temple site with a more bulbous dome. Schedel further enriched his publication by incorporating woodcuts of the Temple from the *Postillae* of Nicolaus de Lyra, published by Koberger in 1481 (fol. LXVIr, v), and these, as discussed in chapter two, show the persistence of an earlier mediaeval tradition.

Surprisingly, this Christian iconographic type of the Temple, based on what is often erroneously described as the Mosque of Omar and more correctly designated the Dome of the Rock, also influenced Jewish pictorial representation of the Temple. This is seen in the Frankfurt *Mishneh Torah* of c. 1450, now in a New York private collection, and is found as late as the Venice Haggadah of 1740, which shows Jerusalem with the Dome of the Rock, representing the Jewish Temple, in a central position.[7] The Venetian print was frequently reproduced in later periods, a similar design appearing in a curtain for the Torah shrine in the Jewish Museum, New York. A number of Polish synagogues, now destroyed, showed related mural decorations that included the city of Jerusalem with the Dome of the Rock. Decorations of similar composition were the work of Eliezer Sussmann ben Solomon Katz from Brody who worked in Germany (c. 1740) in the Synagogue of Horb (now in the Israel Museum, Jerusalem) in 1735; in Schwäbisch-Hall, where they are still found, dated 1739; and in Bechhofen (1733), unfortunately destroyed. A fourth synagogue, from Kirchheim, preserved in the Luitpold Museum, Würzburg, was destroyed, ironically by American bombers in the war of 1939–45.[8] A similar octagonal type influenced the frontispiece of Israel Isserlein's *Terumat ha-Deshen* (Venice 1546) and the colophon to Jonah ben Abraham Gerondi's *Iggeret ha-Teshuvah* of 1595, published in Prague.

*ILL. 57*

*ILL. 61*

*ILL. 62*

*ILL. 64*
*ILL. 65*

*ILL. 63*

*ILL. 59*

The polygonal architectural tradition still influenced Goethe when in the *Paedagogical Province* of *Wilhelm Meister's Travels* (book II, chapter 2) he described a 'round, or rather, octagonal building', which is not explained further but which is connected with a hall. This hall contains paintings representing the Old Testament, while another hall, also adjacent to an open space, shows illustrations of the New Testament. There seems to be a tacit suggestion of the Dome of the Rock, because of the octagonal form of the building coupled with representations of biblical narrative.

It may also be more than fortuitous that Sulpice Boisserée's (1786–1851) reconstruction of the Dome of the Grail is a central building reminiscent of the Holy Sepulchre or the Dome of the Rock, although his High Gothic style is based clearly on the Cathedral of Cologne.[9]

*ILL. 68*
*ILL. 69*

Another successful attempt at realistic interpretation, based on the French environment but nurtured by scriptural and literary traditions, was made after 1470 by the famous painter Jean Foucquet, a native of Tours. He and his disciples reproduced the Jewish Temple in what they regarded as a realistic form, as can be clearly seen in their manuscript of the *Antiquités Judaïques* by Josephus in the Bibliothèque Nationale.[10] They envisaged the structure as a richly decorated late Gothic French church, adding to the façade, however, two turrets crowned by bulbous oriental-looking domes. The entry of Ptolemy into Jerusalem depicts this group of buildings with the Temple in the background. Characteristic

*ILL. 70*

*ILL. 71*

of Foucquet's idiom is the setting of a small town seen within an undulating landscape, giving a realistic impression based on French local colour but also endowing the scene with a sense of fantasy inspired by the orient. Any similarity to the Cathedral of Tours is fortuitous, since the domes on the twin towers of the façade of Tours belong to the mainstream of the Renaissance and are of a later date than Foucquet's illuminations. The same is true of the two domes on the twin towers of the Frauenkirche, Munich.

*ILL. 72*     Particularly interesting is the representation of the interior, which shows Pompey inside the Temple. A slender Ark and the two Cherubim are clearly described and are reminiscent of earlier mediaeval illuminations. They are set against monumental twisted columns, an innovation derived from the 'columnae vitineae', columns decorated with vine leaves, although the vine leaves were in fact omitted. Another illumination from this series also shows the Temple interior in which six columns and the Ark are visible. The scene is the entry of Herod, with a pool for dipping the sick in the foreground and the exterior of the Temple in the left background. This recalls the earlier mediaeval continuous compositions in which various scenes are combined in one picture. It is also interesting to note that in the Boccaccio MS in Munich the definition of pictorial space in the form of a lozenge is characteristic of Foucquet. One illumination, attributed to Foucquet, in this manuscript showing the *lit de justice* of the *Trial of Vendôme*, which took place in 1458, was still used as a prototype for the representation of Jerusalem in the Koberger and subsequent editions of Nicolaus de Lyra (Koberger II, 183v).

As Foucquet visited Rome, he may well have seen the Constantinian columns of old St. Peter's that legend claimed were part of the Solomonic Temple. This is not totally unreasonable because, as is well known, Jewish spoils were transferred to Rome at the destruction of the Temple *ILL. 2*     and are represented on the Arch of Titus. As to Foucquet's Temple columns, they are probably not copies of the ancient ones, as Ward Perkins suggests,[11] but structures in their own right, massive and without vine leaves, whereas the authentic Roman columns were slender and relatively small. Later, Raphael used the motif of twisted columns in one of his famous cartoons, now in the Victoria and Albert Museum, London, including the columns in the scene of *The Healing of the Lame at* *ILL. 73*     *the Beautiful Gate*.[12] Bernini, in the seventeenth century, introduced the motif of the twisted columns twice in his work at St. Peter's, using new pillars in his monumental baldacchino and re-using older ones in the balconies decorating the pillars supporting the dome. The latter were regarded as belonging to Solomon's Temple in the later Middle Ages.[13] Ettlinger draws attention to an interesting point. The paintings of the wall of the Sistine Chapel at the Vatican, built by Pope Sixtus IV between 1471 and 1484, represent Moses and Christ cycles.[14] They therefore express the papal claim to the universal priesthood, seen as foreshadowed by Moses and applied to the papacy. This explains why *The Charge of St. Peter*, a painting by Perugino of 1481–82, is included in the sequence. *ILL. 75* It depicts the Temple as a polygonal building, reminiscent of the Dome of the Rock, in the middle ground, adorned by two porticoes and flanked by two triumphal arches. A similar building is seen in Perugino's *Sposalizio*, the marriage of the Virgin, in Caen, undated but presumably preceding *ILL. 77* Raphael's treatment of the same subject in the Brera, Milan, of 1504. *ILL. 78*

The clarity of elevations and the polygonal outline suggest some fusion of the central architectural Renaissance tradition with the Dome of the Rock on the Temple site. It is from this tradition that the biblical woodcuts attributed to Hans Holbein the younger are derived: they were published in *Historiarum Veteris Testamenti Icones* etc. (Lyons 1539) in Latin and French. Holbein is mentioned by name in the poem in *Historiarum* by *ILL. 74* Nicolaus Borbonius.[15] The Temple is illustrated in the British Library copy of *Historiarum* relating to 'Numbers II' and is used for the depiction of the Tabernacle, standing among the tents of the tribes. A similar prototype of a central building is used for the *Historiarum* illustrations to *Isaiah* 6 and *Ezekiel* 47. The centrepiece is a view of Jerusalem, still derived from Nicolaus de Lyra (Koberger II, fol. 183v). The edition of *Historiarum* of 1538 in the British Library (36 d. 1) has only the Latin text and a derivation from Koberger II, fol. 174, for the illustration to *Ezekiel* 40. There are, as is to be expected, other variations in the different editions of the woodcuts as well.

The same pictorial tradition of a polygonal Temple still informed Rembrandt in the seventeenth century and is seen, for instance, in the so-called *David and Absalom* in the Hermitage, Leningrad (Bredius cat. *ILL. 76* no. 511). The painting by Rembrandt in Edinburgh, representing perhaps *Hannah Teaching Samuel* (Bredius cat. no. 577), shows a universal sanc- *ILL. 130* tuary rather than a specific building, but suggests a polygonal shape, as do many of Rembrandt's other Temple representations.[16]

As to Jewish wall paintings, illuminations, woodcuts and embroideries, the polygonal building is sometimes seen here too, and a Messianic overtone suggested, especially when the prophet Elijah, the forerunner of the Messiah, is depicted riding on a donkey.[17] The same tradition is found in pilgrims' illustrated itineraries.[18] *ILL. 67*

When comparing realism in Jewish and Christian art, the relationship is a close one. However, in Islamic art the emphasis on naturalism in the *ILL. 79* depiction of holy sites was far more pronounced in those geographic regions that allowed figural representation. It was from the Temple site, according to legend, that Mohammed ascended to heaven on his horse, El Burak, and this testifies to the sanctity of the location for his 'night journey'. A good example of a topographical nature is the picture in the British Library (Add. MS 27566) of the Ka'ba ('the black stone') in Mecca, found in the attestation of a pilgrimage by Maimunah, of the year 836 of the Hegira, the flight of Mohammed from Mecca to Medina, equivalent to A.D. 1433. Here the emphasis is entirely on verisimilitude, even the wall 'al-hatim' partially surrounding the Ka'ba is included, as well as the black stone itself, the wall not having been entered during circumambulation. What is set before us is a legal document, different from and opposed to a visionary approach. Indeed, the Ka'ba was never illustrated in the Koran itself, and its pictorial form was only developed in the fifteenth century.[19]

*ILL. 80*

To sum up the position with regard to the Temple tradition in the late Gothic period and its influence: when an interest in detailed realism prevailed, historical and theological considerations receded into the background. So, realistic pictorial interpretations of the Temple dealt with the Dome of the Rock on the Temple site, without raising any historical questions, and for this reason, such interpretations are further removed from a true understanding than the traditional approach based on scripture.

## References

1   E. Lambert, *L'architecture des Templiers* (Paris 1955), *passim*.
2   Cf. e.g. M. Ruston, *Holy Sepulchre Church: The Round Church, Cambridge* (n.d.), Pitkin Pictorial English Churches series, no. 2, p. 10.
3   W. de G. Birch, *Catalogue of Seals in the Department of Manuscripts in the British Museum* (London 1898), vol. V, no. 21083. See note 1 above.
4   E. Panofsky, *Early Netherlandish Painting* (Cambridge, Massachusetts 1953), pp. 230 ff. Cf. P. Durrieu, *Mélanges . . . G. Schlumberger,* vol. II (1924), pp. 506 ff.
5   F. Landsberger in *Jewish Art* (ed. C. Roth) (London 1961), cols. 409–10 and 417–18; B. Narkiss (ed.), *Picture History of Jewish Civilization* (Jerusalem and New York 1970), pp. 188 ff.
6   E. Geck, *Bernhard von Breydenbach, Die Reise ins Heilige Land* (Wiesbaden 1961).
7   B. Narkiss, *Hebrew Illuminated Manuscripts, op. cit.*, pl. 60; R. Wischnitzer-Bernstein, *Symbole und Gestalten der Jüdischen Kunst* (Berlin 1935), p. 125; C. H. Krinsky, *op. cit.,* pp. 1 ff.
8   *Encyclopaedia Judaica*, entry on 'Synagogue', also 'Messiah'.
9   P. Frankl, *The Gothic* (Princeton 1960), pp. 181 ff. and 757. See Boisserée's *Titurel.*
10   P. Durrieu, *Les Antiquités Judaïques et le peintre Jehan Foucquet* (Paris 1908) is still the standard work; cf. also G. T. Cox, *Jehan Foucquet, Native of Tours* (London 1931) and P. Wescher, *Jehan Foucquet and his Time* (London 1947). On the lozenge type of perspective that influenced the Koberger edition of Nicolaus

de Lyra and subsequent works in its representation of Jerusalem cf. O. Pächt in *Journal of the Warburg and Courtauld Institutes*, vol. IV (1940/41), pp. 85 ff.

11 J. Ward Perkins in *Journal of Roman Studies*, vol. 42 (1952), pp. 21 ff.; J. Toynbee and J. Ward Perkins, *The Shrine of St. Peter in Rome and the Vatican Excavations* (London 1956), with full bibliography, esp. pp. 202 and 252.

12 J. Pope-Hennessy, *Victoria and Albert Museum: The Raphael Cartoons* (London 1950); J. Shearman, *Raphael's Cartoons* etc. (London 1972).

13 R. Wittkower, *Art and Architecture in Italy, 1600–1750* (Harmondsworth 1958), pp. 115 and 347.

14 L. D. Ettlinger, *The Sistine Chapel before Michelangelo* (Oxford 1965), *passim*.

15 H. A. Schmid, *Hans Holbein der Jüngere* (Basel 1945–48), especially vol. II.

16 A. Bredius, *Rembrandt* (H. Gerson, ed.) (3rd edn.: London 1969), nos. 511 and 577.

17 R. Wischnitzer-Bernstein, *Symbole und Gestalten der Jüdischen Kunst* (Berlin 1935), pp. 124 f.

18 R. Barnett in *Journal of Jewish Art*, vol. II (1975), pp. 28 ff.

19 *The Encyclopaedia of Islam*, entry for 'Ka'ba' by A. J. Wensinck; R. Ettinghausen, *Arabic Painting* (Cleveland, Ohio 1962), especially pp. 41 ff. Ettinghausen deals with the problem of Moslem realism in general. Priscilla Soucek in *The Temple of Solomon, op. cit.*, pp. 73 ff.

53 Seal of the Templars, appended to an Act of 1255 (London, British Museum, Birch V, 18913)

54 Seal of Father Andreas de Coloors of the Templars, appended to an Act of 1214 (London, British Museum, Birch V, 21083)

**55**  Hartmann Schedel, *Liber Cronicarum*, view of the Temple, with bulbous dome decorated by crescent representing *Templum Salomonis* (London, British Library)

**56**  Hartmann Schedel, *Liber Cronicarum*, view of Jerusalem, showing Temptation on the left (London, British Library)

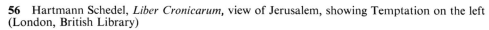

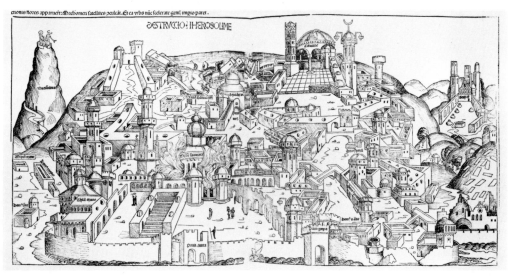

(*opposite*)
**57** Maimonides, *Mishneh Torah*, view of the Temple suggested by the Dome of the Rock, flanked by two figures, sacrificing (New York, private collection)

(*above*)
**58** Barend van Orley (attributed to), *The Crucifixion,* detail showing a central building vaguely reminiscent of the Colosseum. Van Orley was a well-known Romanist (photograph by courtesy of Agnew's, London)

(*right*)
**59** Israel Isserlein, *Terumat ha-Deshen* (a collection of responsa), view of the Temple (London, British Library)

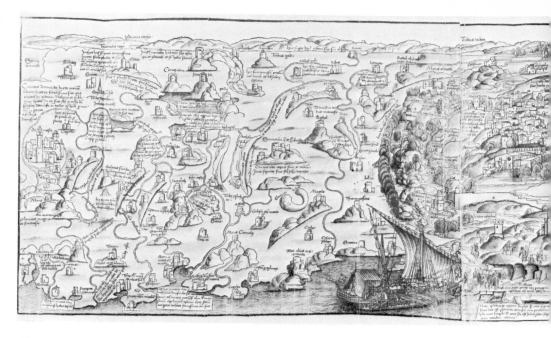

**60** Bernhard von Breydenbach, *Peregrinatio,* folding plate showing general view of Jerusalem and other places (London, British Library)

**61** Venice Haggadah showing Messianic vision of Jerusalem, with numerous figures including the Prophet, preceded by Herald blowing the *shofar*

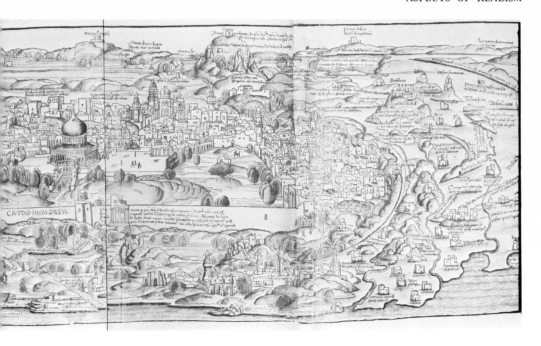

**62** Curtain showing view of Jerusalem (New York, Jewish Museum)

(*opposite*)
**63** Synagogue of Kirchheim, interior with wall painting showing view of Jerusalem, now destroyed

(*above*)
**64** Synagogue of Horb, wall painting showing view of Jerusalem (Jerusalem, Israel Museum)

(*right*)
**65** Synagogue of Schwäbisch-Hall, detail of wall painting showing view of Jerusalem

**66** Nineteenth-century *sukkah* (Jewish structure connected with the Feast of Tabernacles) from Fischach, interior with wall painting showing view of Jerusalem in a folk art style (Jerusalem, Israel Museum)

**67** Embroidery showing the itinerary for Jewish pilgrims (Jerusalem, Israel Museum)

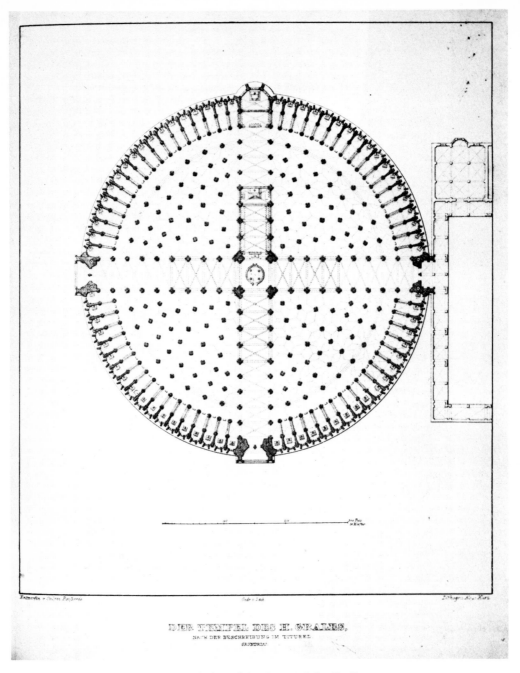

DER TEMPEL DES H. GRALES,
NACH DER BESCHREIBUNG IM TITUREL
GRUNDRISS

**68** Sulpice Boisserée, *Titurel,* ground plan of the Dome of the Grail

**69** Sulpice Boisserée, *Titurel,* elevation of the Dome of the Grail

**70** Jean Foucquet, *Antiquités Judaïques,* conquest of Jerusalem by Nebuzar-Adan (Paris, Bibliothèque Nationale)

(*opposite*)
**71** Jean Foucquet, *Antiquités Judaïques,* entry of Ptolemy Soter (Paris, Bibliothèque Nationale)

Uant alixandre roy
des macedoniens eust
restauut le royaume des
perssiens et ordonne in
dre et quil mourut il laissa moult de
successeurs. Car antigon prist asie.

Seleucus prist babiloine et les ars
denviron. Lisimacus tint lellespont.
Cassander conquist macedoine.
Ptholomee filz de lagi possten egipte.
Et ainsi comme tous ceulx a
avoient discenaon entre eulx et que

Ons auons moustre
au uolume de dauant
cestuy a la mort de la
royne alexandre. Or
racomptons les choses qui sensuiuet
et ne tendons a nulle autre chose for:

a riens trespasser des choses qui ont
este faictes en puniteant ala memo
ire de ceulx qui les liront. Car a
ceulx qui escripuant hystoires ou ra
comptent choses anciennes il conui
ent pour lanciennete mettre ou faire

**73**  Raphael, *Healing of the Lame at the Beautiful Gate* (London, Victoria and Albert Museum)

(*opposite*)
**72**  Jean Foucquet, *Antiquités Judaïques,* Pompey in the Temple (Paris, Bibliothèque Nationale)

**74**  Hans Holbein the younger (?), *The Temple Surrounded by Tents of the Israelites* (London, British Museum)

75  Perugino, *The Charge of St. Peter* (Rome, Sistine Chapel)

(*below left*) 76  Rembrandt, *David and Absalom* (Leningrad, Hermitage Museum)

(*below right*) 77  Perugino, *Sposalizio* or *The Marriage of the Virgin* (Caen, Musée des Beaux-Arts)

(*opposite*) 78  Raphael, *Sposalizio* or *The Marriage of the Virgin* (Milan, Pinacoteca di Brera)

**80**  Document with representation of Ka'ba in Mecca, 1433 (London, British Library,
Add. MS 27566)

(*opposite*)
**79**  The Prophet Mohammed's vision of an angel's presentation of Temple Precincts
(Istanbul, Topkapi Sarayi Müzesi Kütüphanesi, Hazine 2154, 107)

**81** Interior of Temple of Lyons in a street called 'Paradise'. Note that most participants are seen with heads covered. (Geneva, University of Geneva)

# CHAPTER IV

# Reformation and Counter-Reformation

DURING THE SIXTEENTH century the Reformation consciously returned to biblical sources and therefore Christian Hebraists rediscovered the biblical tradition in a scientific endeavour to absorb historical truth. This attitude is in striking contrast to the late mediaeval iconography which incorporated realistic contemporary detail into its image of the Temple, oblivious of the fact that the polygonal Temple representation was an Islamic structure.

The Temple of Solomon was reconstructed in the Latin Estienne Bible, published in Paris in 1540. On the title page an acknowledgement is made to the great linguistic scholar Franciscus Vatablus (Waterbled), Professor of Hebrew at the Royal College in Paris, who had been accused of Protestant heresies and who died in 1547: 'To these are added the designs of the Tabernacle of Moses and of the Temple of Solomon [which are presented] with the utmost skill and accuracy following Franciscus Vatablus.' ('His accesserunt schemata Tabernaculi Mosaici et Templi Salomonis quae praeeunte Francisco Vatablo . . . summa arte et fide expressa sunt.') These words obviously do not refer to the anonymous and rather clumsy craftsman who executed the illustrations, but to the mind that inspired them.[1] The many illustrations that illuminate the text of the Estienne Bible are indeed astonishing. The Temple is seen first with
*ILL. 82* its roof removed, a Mannerist device, probably Vatablus's idea, thus allowing the view of the Ark and the Cherubim, as well as the two columns, Jachin and Boaz, free-standing before the façade (fol. 15r and v). This
*ILL. 83* image is followed by a more conventional view of the Temple with a flat roof, preceded by the adjoining courts. This principle of eliminating the roof is also applied to the Tabernacle (fol. 28) while the side wall is removed from the Hall of the Cedars of Lebanon (fol. 117, the top schema).

Vatablus continued the work on scripture initiated by the Protestant Leo Juda or Judä (1482–1542), an Alsatian and a friend of Zwingli. Vatablus was understandably accused of Protestant leanings. As to Leo Juda, his son, Johannes Jud, called Leu, mentioned without apparent misgivings a possibility of a Jewish ancestry.[2] He also commented on the many Jews living in Alsace. This fact indeed makes Jewish antecedents likely. Johannes Leu added that to be regarded as Jewish was not shameful, as to be born a son of Abraham physically was good, although it was even better to have become a son of Abraham spiritually.[3] This statement is reminiscent of Maimonides's favourable attitude to proselytes.

The façade inspired by Vatablus is substantially correct when compared with Busink's recent, learned reconstructions of Solomon's Temple (Avi Yonah's popular reconstruction refers to Herod's Temple). It gained great popularity and influenced the reconstruction of the Jewish Temple in the seventeenth century by Claude Perrault, the famous architect of the Louvre in Paris. Perrault was the illustrator of the code of Maimonides, the *Mishneh Torah*, which had been translated into Latin and published in 1678 by Louis Compiègne de Veil, a Catholic convert of Jewish origin.[4] *ILLS. 85, 86*

At an earlier date, Leone Battista Alberti (1404–1472), in his *De Re Aedificatoria* of 1452, first printed in 1485, had shown little interest in the Jewish tradition. He favoured the circular form and designated churches as 'temples'. He considered the Altar of Hewn Stone to be barbarous (book VII, chapter V) but referred (book VII, chapter XIII) with approval to a candlestick similar to one described in the Bible (see chapter II). *ILL. 87* Here it should be remembered that this candelabrum had a long iconographic history in Jewish and Christian illuminated manuscripts and was illustrated both in the Estienne Bible and in the French translation of *De Re Aedificatoria*, entitled *L'architecture et art de bien bastir . . .* by the learned physician Jean Martin, posthumously published in Paris in 1553. The circular form for churches, as we have seen, was familiar during the Middle Ages from the Church of the Holy Sepulchre and the Dome of the Rock, adapted as a church by the Templars.

However, there is another tradition for the use of the word 'temple' to describe a Christian church. It was Calvin (1509–1564) who first introduced it for the churches following his own persuasion in Switzerland and France, establishing in this manner not only his challenge to the Roman Church but also the primacy of his religious leadership as a continuation of the ancient priesthood. One of these temples, originally a private house, existed in Lyons from 1564 until the French Revolution, although then *ILL. 81* it was no longer used as a place of worship. A painting, now at the University of Geneva, depicts this temple accurately, with its seats for women, separated from those for the men. The gallery at Lyons, as in other Protestant churches, however, was not used as a separate part allotted to women, as found in post-mediaeval Orthodox synagogues. The different activities in the temple, e.g. baptism, marriage and preaching, are portrayed.[5]

Jacques Perret, a 'Savoyard gentleman' as he described himself, designed three different types of Protestant temples in his *Des fortifications et artifices* published in Frankfurt in 1602. The small, middle-sized and

ILL. 88   large buildings, basically conceived in a sober and functional style, show the division in seating between men and women of different ranks and, except in the small one, places are allotted to seigneurs and their ladies, while galleries are provided for the lower orders. Perret showed his buildings with and without roofs, and also suggested wistfully that the large temple could easily be adapted to some secular use, such as a town hall (plates H, O, X). It was Perret, in addition, who designed a skyscraper palace for a prince, perhaps to facilitate defence in troubled times, replacing the customary horizontal layout with a vertical one.

The most famous of the Protestant temples actually built was the one in Charenton, near Paris, first erected in 1606, destroyed by fanatics in

ILL. 89   1621 and rebuilt by Salomon de Brosse in 1622–23, only to be destroyed again by religious enemies in 1686.[6] According to A. Furetière in the Temple entry of volume IV of the *Dictionnaire universel* (1727): 'By the Edicts of Pacification the French Reformed [Church] members were entitled to have a certain number of Temples in each province, but all these Temples have been demolished, following diverse regulations, and in the end, by an Edict given in 1685.' He also mentioned Hungary, where 'malcontents' wanted to re-establish their temples. It is interesting to note that a 'church' in Hungarian is called a *templom*; plural, *templomok*.

The Chevalier Louis de Jaucourt pointed out, in the Temple article from Diderot and d'Alembert's *Encyclopédie*, published in 1765, that the terms 'temple' and 'church' are synonymous; the word 'church' ('église') he considered more usual, but not when applied to Protestant places of worship.

It is in this Protestant succession that Matthias Hafenreffer's reconstructions of the Temple are placed. The image of the Temple in his book

ILL. 90   *Templum Ezechielis*, published in Tübingen in Germany in 1613, displays the ornate forms characteristic of the *ohrmuschel* or 'earlobe' style, so called because emphasis is placed on convoluted and complicated forms; they are more accentuated than they are in Perret. Hafenreffer was an orthodox Protestant who combined instruction with a Lutheran interpretation of the Bible as a Professor of Theology and Chancellor of Tübingen University. He located the Palace of Solomon behind the Temple in an axial arrangement, and there is no reason to suppose that he was influenced by any but his own beliefs and motivations, eccentric as they were.

It is also from the Protestant tradition that Dutch synagogues were architecturally derived. The most famous of these is the Portuguese

93

Synagogue in Amsterdam, based on the Protestant Temple of Charenton near Paris. Among the characteristic structural details of the Temple at Charenton were the large columns running without interruption through the lower galleries to support the upper ones, a motif based on Vitruvius (V : 6). This feature was developed further in the Portuguese Synagogue of Amsterdam in which the women's gallery, supported by small columns, is relegated to the outer aisles so as not to break the lines of the large round pillars that carry the vault.[7] The Dutch arrangement appeared in England on a more restricted scale in the Portuguese Synagogue of London, begun in 1701, and was structurally more pronounced in the later Great Synagogue of London of 1790, the decoration of which was in the Adam style. In the Great Synagogue, damaged during the 1939–45 war and now *ILL. 142* destroyed, the pillars supporting the women's gallery carried through to the ceiling without interruption.[8]

The formal tradition of the Italian Renaissance is seen in the illustrations of the work connected with Benedictus Arias Montanus (1527–1598), *Exemplar siue de sacris fabricis liber* in the Polyglot Bible of 1572, vol. *ILL. 91* VIII ff., although Montanus's significance has been overshadowed by the later and more visionary reconstructions of Villalpando, which will be discussed below. The *Exemplar* was also published in Leiden in 1593, as a single volume work *Antiquitatum Iudaicarum* (libri IX etc. . .). Montanus, a scholar and diplomat, tried to combine in an active life the pursuits of research in a setting of tolerance.[9] He worked for peace during the religious wars in Flanders and was accused of Judaizing by Leon de Castro of Salamanca because he favoured the original biblical text rather than the Vulgate. He attended the Council of Trent in 1562, collaborated in the polyglot edition of the Bible, as stated above, and was entrusted by Philip II with the supervision of the library of the Escorial. Montanus reconstructed the Temple according to the Hebrew tradition with a tower above the porch in a formal pattern according to Nicolaus de Lyra, but gave five storeys to the elevation. He was greatly interested in the location of the tribal tents and in the Tabernacle, representing the *ILL. 92* Cherubim as small child-like *putti* decorating the curtains of the Taber- *ILL. 93* nacle. He also elaborately reconstructed Noah's Ark and showed a design of Christ, with stigmata, in a coffin of identical proportions, thus *ILL. 94* stressing the mystical element in salvation. A topographical map is also *ILL. 95* included.

The next step, a far-reaching one, in the presentation of the Temple image was taken by the two Spanish Jesuits, Hieronymo Prado (1547–1595) and Juan Bautista Villalpando (1552–1608), the former more of a biblical scholar, the latter more aesthetically inclined. The three volumes of their *In Ezechielem Explanationes*, published in Rome between 1594 and 1605, are amply illustrated, especially the second volume, for which Villalpando was solely responsible.

ILLS. 98, 99, 123

The Temple ground plan, situated in a regular square symmetrically divided into nine courts, is reminiscent of the Escorial and may show the influence of Juan de Herrera, the chief architect of the Escorial, who is considered to have been a Lullite and mystic. At any rate, Villalpando was equally interested in the architectural elements of Vitruvian models, and it should not be forgotten that the main purpose of the treatise was Christian and biblical, the interpretation of Ezekiel's visions.[10]

ILL. 97

Villalpando still reconstructed the elevation of the eastern façade according to II *Chronicles* 3: 4, the measurement reaching 120 cubits by including the height of the pediment. The monumental infra-structure with deep niches, which acts as a support for the Temple courts, possibly might have been reflected in the basement of the Adelphi in London, designed in 1768–72 by the Adam brothers on a site facing the Thames.[11] An elaborate

ILL. 95

map of Jerusalem including detailed reconstructions is seen in Villalpando's third volume (after fol. 68), but it should not be forgotten that a simpler map was already available in Montanus's work and that both plans are indebted to attempts of the Roman Renaissance at archaeological

ILL. 96

research.[12] The plans of both Montanus and Villalpando show historical sites in classical style; no doubt the plans of Jerusalem were not only influenced by topographical and antiquarian studies but also by designs showing Roman locations. At the same time Villalpando quotes the work of Jewish sages, especially that of David Kimche.

ILL. 100

Particularly strange are the Seraphim-like beings that are amalgamated with the Cherubim by Villalpando and based on *Ezekiel* 41: 18 and *Isaiah* 6: 2. The four faces of each of these Seraphim-like beings cannot but be regarded symbolically, expressing *prudentia*, *fortitudo*, *justitia* and *temperantia* (vol. II, fol. 318). Villalpando maintained, however, that the feet of these creatures were like 'the sole of a calf's foot', and this is clearly shown on the engraving representing the interior of the Holy of Holies (*Ezekiel* 1: 7). He accepted that the tall angel-like beings alternated with palm trees and suggested in effect that their human faces looked inwards towards the Ark, and their leonine faces outwards. Villalpando regarded this arrangement as equivalent to that belonging to the Cherubim of the Temple. He also saw the Temple vision of Ezekiel as a paradigm or classical prototype. It represented perfection, being based on God's own design, and this quality Villalpando also found in the teaching of Vitruvius, which he regarded as classical. Furthermore, Solomon's and Ezekiel's Temples were bound to be identical, according to Villalpando, as they were based on divine guidance and, for him, this necessitated geometric regularity.

G. Surenhusius's famous *Mischna* edition (Amsterdam 1698–1705), *ILLS. 106, 107* especially volume V containing the tractate *Middoth*, is just one outstanding example of Villalpando's influence, as many of the illustrations, especially the depiction of the façade, are indebted to the Spanish architectural model, more particularly some designed by C. Huyberts.[13] Surenhusius also included in his illustrations the plan by L'Empereur which shows the asymmetrical position of the Temple on a folding map in *ILL. 108* *Middoth* (C. L'Empereur, *Talmudis Babylonici Codex Middoth*, Leiden 1630). Wenzel Hollar's simplified copies after Villalpando also testify to the popularity of the illustrations without, however, revealing a more personal adaptation (*Biblia Sacra Polyglotta*, ed. R. Walton, London 1657).

Perhaps the most interesting personal interpretation of Villalpando's prototypes was the work of the Dutch engraver and writer Jan (or Johannes) Luyken or Luiken (1645–1712) especially his *Afbeeldingen der* *ILL. 101* *merkwaardigste Geschiedenissen van het Oude en Nieuwe Testament . . .* of 1729. It was also published in French with the original engravings and added French captions in Amsterdam in 1732, and shows in one of the numerous plates (no. 30 left) the Temple, in Villalpando's classicizing style but preceded by the free-standing columns Jachin and Boaz, which characterize Solomon's Temple. He was possibly influenced in this motif by Matthaeus Merian (1593–1650), the celebrated topographer and engraver (see p. 135). At any rate Luyken's style is highly individual, a picturesque interpretation of the Baroque, with plentiful introductions of striking effects of light and an emphasis on diagonal compositions.

It is also to the Villalpando tradition, although much coarsened and simplified, that a folding map of Jerusalem in a posthumous edition of 1681, the *Itinerarium per Palaestinam*, belongs. The author was Leonhard Rauwolf, whose pseudonym appears as Leo Flaminius. He was a Lutheran, *ILL. 102* botanist, physician and traveller (c. 1535/45–1596) and had travelled widely in the Middle East.[14] The plate seems older than the book, and differs greatly from the other conventional geographic maps included therein. At any rate, it shows some classicizing features, reminiscent of Villalpando's map, including an amphitheatre. On the other hand, the *ILL. 96* margins of the print relate New Testament events, such as the Crucifixion, which are only mentioned, but not included in the far more sophisticated and systematic map of Villalpando. The spirit of the Counter-Reformation continued to pervade the Baroque, based at least partially on Villalpando's influence. A few examples could evoke the process. It should be remembered that de la Ruffinière du Prey has drawn attention to the University Church of Sant' Ivo della Sapienza, Rome, by Borromini (1599–1667), which includes palm-trees and Cherubim, following Villal- *ILL. 103* pando, in its decoration and also has a ground plan in the shape of a hexagon, possibly derived, according to the author, from the *sigillium Salomonis*, the seal of Solomon. This is not impossible, although the pentagram was also considered to have been the seal of Solomon, and the *magen* David, the six-pointed star called the shield of David, became more popular as an emblem of Judaism as the age progressed.[15]

The most outstanding follower of Villalpando was perhaps the celebrated Austrian architect, Johann Bernhard Fischer von Erlach (1656–1723), whose famous work, *Entwürff einer Historischen Architectur* etc., meant to be a comprehensive survey of the history of architecture, published in German as well as in French, appeared first in 1721 and was translated into English in 1737 from the second edition of 1725. He not only reproduced Villalpando's Temple ground plan and elevations but saw its architecture in an historical setting, including in his study the Tower of Babel, pyramids and Chinese palaces and also some of his own

ILLS. 104, 105 work, notably the Church of St. Charles Borromaeus (the Karlskirche) in Vienna, built from 1716 onwards. The façade of this church is enriched by two free-standing columns, most likely a reminiscence of the columns of Solomon's Temple, Jachin and Boaz. In view of Fischer von Erlach's historical interests and these unusual motifs, a biblical influence is suggested, characteristically couched in Baroque exuberance.[16]

Sir Isaac Newton (1643–1727), the famous physicist, was also engaged in religious and biblical speculation. He was interested not only in the chronology of ancient empires but also in the exact measurements of the

ILL. 109 Jewish Temple, to which he devoted a treatise, *A Description of the Temple of Solomon*, forming chapter V (pp. 332 ff.) of his *Chronology of Ancient Kingdoms Amended*, published by John Conduitt in London in 1728. Newton's interest was not primarily architectural: indeed, he placed the Temple symmetrically within the square court, thus ignoring the Jewish tradition as popularized by L'Empereur and Templo (see p. 134 f.).

By contrast, outstanding among those who appreciated an architectural relationship between the Temple and the Tabernacle was the Oratorian priest Bernard Lamy (1640–1715), known for his interests in philosophy, science and mathematics. An unorthodox thinker and a follower of Malebranche, he ran into trouble with the doctors of the Sorbonne, while his friendship with Arnauld and his leanings towards the Jansenists also made him suspect. Nevertheless, he was highly regarded and honoured within his Order.

Lamy's monumental work, *De Tabernaculo Foederis, de sancta Civitate Jerusalem et de Templo ejus* was lovingly, although posthumously, published in Paris by his fellow Oratorian, Louis Ellies Du Pin in 1720.[17] This reconstruction of the Temple differs radically from that of Villalpando, whom Lamy mentioned with scant respect. Lamy attempted to return to the sources; as a rationalist he distrusted symbolism and allegory and was fascinated by historical facts. Therefore he turned again to II *Chronicles* 3:4 and, although he reconstructed the Temple without a tower, still *p. 185* gave an elevation to the façade of 120 cubits (pl. XIX). He thus achieved a *ILL. 111* monumental structure of clear form, an impression apparent not only in the simplified general view but seen more especially in the western aspect which is adorned by a great double staircase of an almost Classical shape. Lamy was also interested in detail, such as the *exedra* of the Hall of Hewn Stone mentioned in the *Mishnah* (Lishkat Hagadol) (pl. XV), reminiscent of the same motif which is found earlier in the ground plan of the Temple Precincts in the *Mishneh Torah* of the fourteenth century in the Jewish Theological Seminary of America, New York (see p. 48). He also included a map of Jerusalem showing the Temple infrastructures, which also inspired other monumental representations. *ILL. 110*

Lamy's skilled engraver was frequently Ferdinand Delamonce, who was interested in structure rather than the detailed fittings and decorations so conspicuous in Villalpando's reconstructions (pl. XIX). Unfortunately, the abundant lettering on the engravings of the Temple plates in Lamy's work does not correspond with the inscriptions specified in his text, nor is it consistent. Furthermore, the Latin captions to the Temple plates, presumably the work of Ellies Du Pin, are somewhat misleading. However, the pillars Jachin and Boaz are prominent and correctly placed. Delamonce was also responsible for depicting the monumental Temple substructures in plate X, derived from, but not identical with, those of Villalpando. *ILL. 112*

Lamy's interpretation of the Tabernacle as a tent with a higher beam supporting the centre was untraditional but is, as it were, realistic because this is, in fact, the usual appearance of a tent. It also helped to emphasize a certain similarity between the elevations of the Tabernacle and of the Temple, although this reconstruction is textually incorrect (pl. V).

Indicative of Lamy's influence is the translation by Richard Bundy, based on the second edition of Lamy's *Introduction à l'écriture sainte* of 1709, entitled *Apparatus Biblicus or an Introduction to the Holy Scriptures,* which appeared in London in 1723. The engravings are by Jacob Pine *ILL. 115* (1690–1756), a follower of Bernard Picard, the well known engraver of Jewish ceremonial life.

Richard Bundy's engravings illustrating biblical episodes elaborate on Lamy's designs for Jerusalem, especially in his indication of the sites of the synagogues, which are shown as tower-like buildings each surmounted by a Jew blowing the *shofar* (opposite his p. 74). He was also *ILL. 114* fascinated by Noah's Ark, which he set in a picturesque landscape (opposite his p. 58).

Perhaps, on a minor scale, a word should be added about Louis Maillet's

Temple reconstructions, published under the title *Les figures du Temple et du palais de Salomon*, in Paris in 1695, as well as about the reconstruction of Solomon's palace, the latter being of particular interest to the author. Maillet, who died in 1720, was a priest and a canon of the Cathedral of Troyes. He was an architectural dilettante and had designed among other buildings the façade of Saint Martin-ès-Vignes, Troyes, now destroyed.[18]

*ILLS. 116, 117*

*p. 185*

*ILLS. 118, 119*

He emphasized symmetry and the height of the rather unwieldy tower of the Temple proper, based on II *Chronicles* 3: 4, but it is with his palace design that Maillet came into his own. The palace and the Hall of the Forest of Lebanon appear as symmetrical units, open to a court in front, while at the back, Maillet's reconstruction of the palace opens on to a garden. This super-Versailles fits the magnificence of Solomon, whom Maillet regarded as a figure similar to Louis XIV.

It should be remembered in this context that numerous Temple illustrations are found in and on the margins of maps, many of them following older prototypes. Herrmann has drawn attention to a volume in the British Library (L. 12. f. 4) which contains a Latin Bible, as well as a great number of unrelated pages in Latin and French. Herrmann sees here partly the work of Desbrulins, who was, however, a calligrapher and not a writer (see 'septième figure'). This *volume factice* contains a few manuscript pages, sections from Latin and French Bibles and from the *Géographie sacrée* of Nicolas Sanson. Some of the illustrations were executed by Delamonce, G. Scotin the elder and Moullart-Sanson. They show a fascinating cross-section of French taste.[19]

During the Reformation, the Counter-Reformation and the Baroque, therefore, Protestant and Catholic scholars collaborated and influenced one another. The Jews were naturally regarded as the keepers of tradition; furthermore, the existence of two rival Christian denominations and the partially maintained humanist outlook gave a wider view of religious diversity than the Middle Ages had known. This could lead to a climate of greater toleration for the Jews, not to be confused with either equality or emancipation, concepts which later came to the fore in the eighteenth century.

### References

1 Discussed in a different context by W. Herrmann in *Essays Presented to Rudolf Wittkower* etc. (London 1967), vol. I, pp. 143 ff. (The order of figs 7 and 8 should be reversed). Also, W. Herrmann, *The Theory of Claude Perrault* (London 1973).

2 'Es hat wohl Manchen fremd bedünkt, dass ein Christ soll heissen Jud . . . Nun mocht es wohl sein dass vielleicht seine Vorfahren wären Juden gewesen . . . besonders weil dort im Elsass viele Juden wohnen.'

3   C. Pestalozzi, *Leo Judä* (Elberfeld 1860), one of the series *Leben der Väter* (introduced by K. R. Hagenbach), see especially p. 2.

4   For an assessment of Perrault see note 1 above.

5   W. Richard, 'Untersuchungen zur Genesis der reformierten Kirchenterminologie der Westschweiz und Frankreichs', *Romanica Helvetica*, vol. 57 (1959), especially pp. 83 ff.; W. Weiss in *Bulletin Historique et Littéraire, Société de l'histoire du Protestantisme Français*, vol. 38/39 (1890), pp. 286 ff.; Baron, vol. XIV, *passim*.

6   J. Pannier, *Salomon de Brosse* (Paris 1911), pp. 86 ff.; R. Coope, *Salomon de Brosse* (London 1972), pp. 183 ff. and *passim*; H. Rosenau in *Journal of the Warburg and Courtauld Institutes,* vol. IV (1940/41), pp. 80 ff.; Wischnitzer, *The European Synagogue, passim.*

7   Rosenau, *Jewish Art*, pp. 38 and 39.

8   Rosenau, see note 7 above.

9   B. Rekers, *Benito Arias Montano (1527–1598)* (London and Leiden 1972).

10  W. Herrmann and R. Taylor in *Essays, op. cit.* (see note 1 above), pp. 143 ff. and 81 ff. respectively.

11  The literature on the Adam brothers is enormous; cf. lately D. Yarwood, *Robert Adam* (London 1970) and R. Oresko, *The Works in Architecture of Robert and James Adam* (London 1975).

12  See M. R. Scherer, *Marvels of Ancient Rome* (New York 1955) for a brief survey.

13  Cornelis Huyberts (or Huybert) was a renowned and prolific engraver (1669/70–1712 or after).

14  K. H. Dannenfeldt, *Leonhard Rauwolf* (Cambridge, Massachusetts 1968).

15  On Borromini cf. P. de la Ruffinière du Prey in *Zeitschrift für Kunstgeschichte,* vol. 31 (1968), pp. 216 ff. Furthermore, Kircher mentioned the 'Shield of Solomon' as one of the two Mohammedan *telesmata*, without any Christian connotation. See also H. Ost in the same periodical, vol. 30 (1967), pp. 101 ff. G. Scholem, *The Messianic Idea in Judaism* (London 1971), pp. 257 ff. A. Blunt in *Kunsthistorische Forschungen Otto Pächt zu seinem 70. Geburtstag* (Salzburg 1972), pp. 258 ff.

16  G. Kunoth, *Die Historische Architektur Fischer von Erlachs* (Düsseldorf 1956).

17  F. Girbal, *Bernard Lamy, 1640–1715* (Paris 1964).

18  Cf. H. Rosenau in *Gazette des Beaux-Arts*, vol. 78 (1971), pp. 307 ff.

19  W. Herrmann in *Essays, op. cit.* (see note 1 above), p. 158, no. 44. L. Bagrow and R. A. Skelton, *History of Cartography* (London 1964), *passim.*

(*opposite*)
**82**  Franciscus Vatablus, *In Ezechielem explanationes et apparatus urbis ac templi Hierosolymitani commentariis et imaginibus illustratus,* interior of the Temple (London, British Library)

(*page 102*)
**83**  Franciscus Vatablus, *In Ezechielem . . . ,* Temple Precincts (London, British Library)

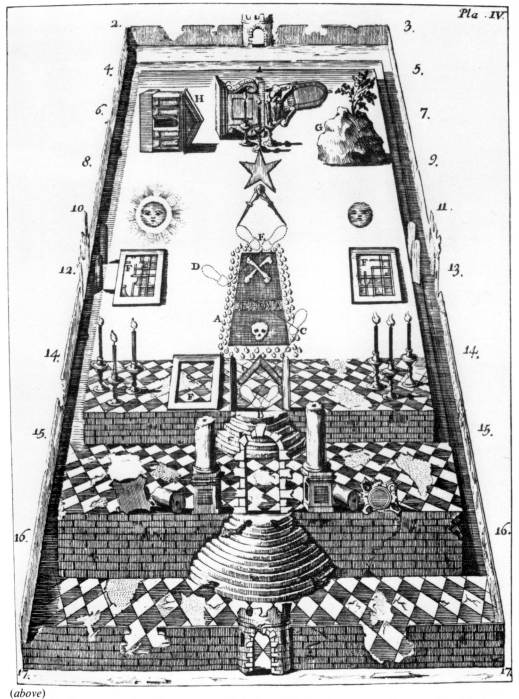

(*above*)
**84** Satirical representation of a Freemason's lodge, 1747, bearing a resemblance to Vatablus's view of the Temple Precincts

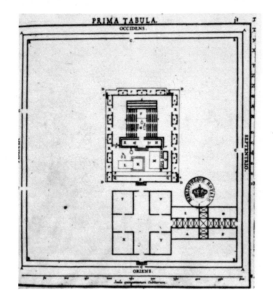

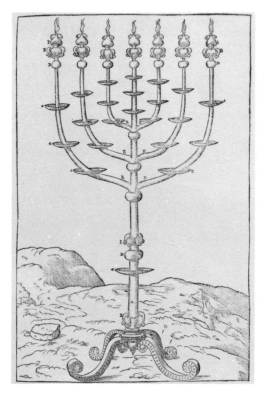

(*above left*)
**85** Claude Perrault, illustration to the code of Maimonides, plan of the Temple (Paris, Bibliothèque Nationale)

(*above right*)
**86** Claude Perrault, illustration to the code of Maimonides, Temple elevation (Paris, Bibliothèque Nationale)

(*left*)
**87** Leone Battista Alberti, *L'architecture* . . . (J. Martin translation), candlestick (London, British Library)

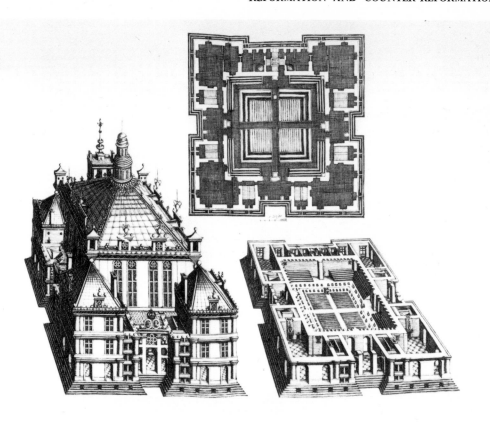

**88** Jacques Perret, *Des Fortifications* . . . , large Protestant temple, possibly designed to be used also as a secular hall (London, British Library)

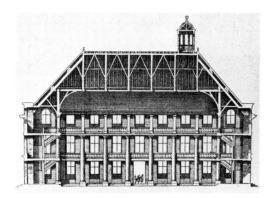

**89** J. Marot, section of the temple in Charenton

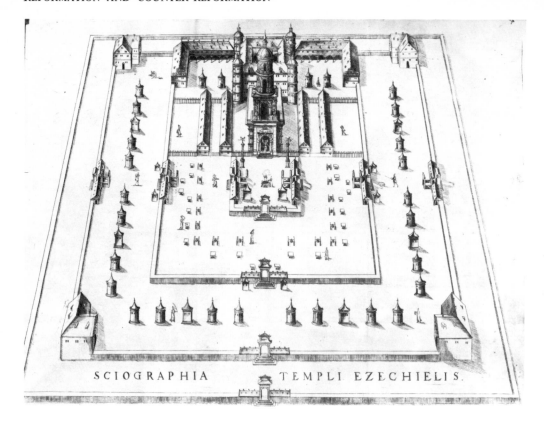

SCIOGRAPHIA TEMPLI EZECHIELIS.

**90** Matthias Hafenreffer, *Templum Ezechielis,* Precincts of the Temple (London, British Library)

SACRÆ ÆDIS ICNOGRAPHIA EX BENEDICTI ARIÆ MONTANI DESCRIPTIONE

TEMPLI CVM PORTICV ET CELLIS ABSOLVTA ORTHOGRAPHIA *ex descriptione* Bened. *Ariæ* Montani.
*Conuenit orthographia cum Icnographia mensuris ad Vnguem. Membra omnia respondent Architecturæ Israelitarum*

**91** Benedictus Arias Montanus, *Exemplar . . .* , elevation and ground plan of the Temple (London, British Library)

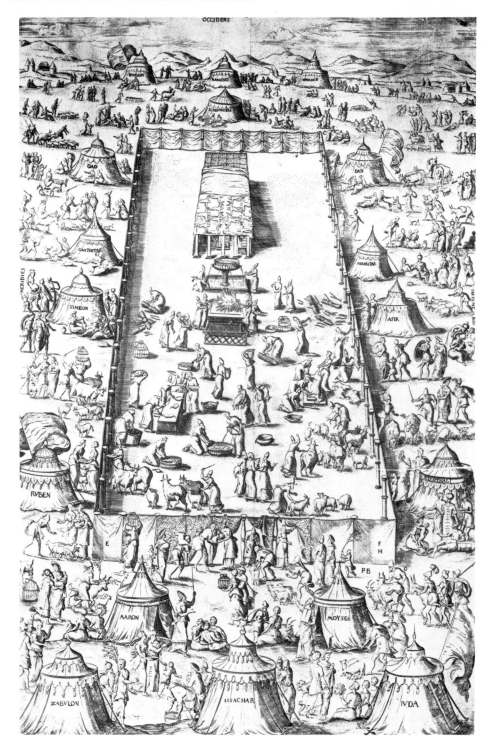

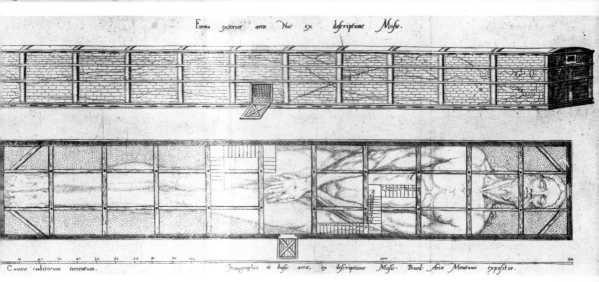

(*opposite*)
**92** Benedictus Arias Montanus, *Exemplar . . .* , activities surrounding the
Tabernacle and tribal tents (London, British Library)

(*top*)
**93** Benedictus Arias Montanus, *Exemplar . . .* , curtains of the Tabernacle with child-like
Cherubim (London, British Library)

(*above*)
**94** Benedictus Arias Montanus, *Exemplar . . .* , Noah's Ark as the coffin of Christ (London,
British Library)

109

**95** Benedictus Arias Montanus, *Exemplar* . . . , Jerusalem in landscape (London, British Library)

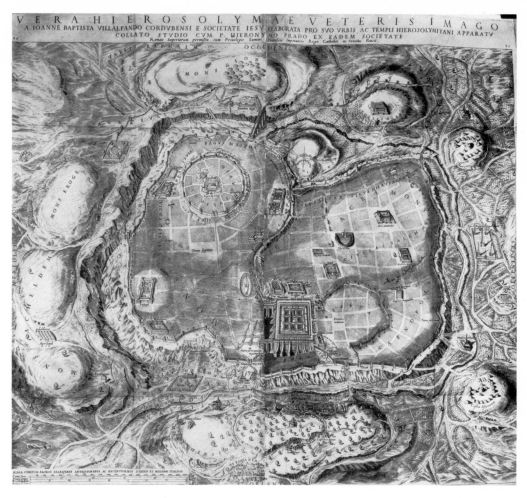

**96** Juan Bautista Villalpando, *In Ezechielem Explanationes,* map of Jerusalem (London, British Library)

VNIVERSI TEMPLI HIEROSOLYMITANI ORTHOGRAPHIA QVAE OSTENDIT ORIENTALEM FA

**97** Juan Bautista Villalpando, *In Ezechielem Explanationes*, folding plate showing Temple elevation (London, British Library)

(*opposite*)
**98** Juan de Herrera, ground plan of the Escorial

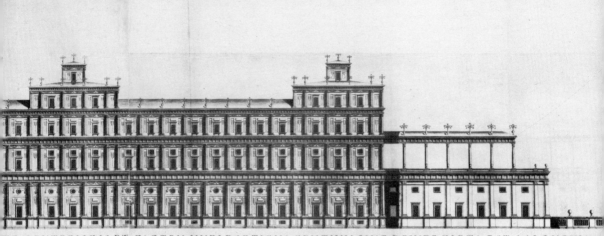

TRII EXTERIORIS ET PARTEM MVRI PORTICVS GENTIVM QVAE DEINDE DICTA EST SALOMONIS

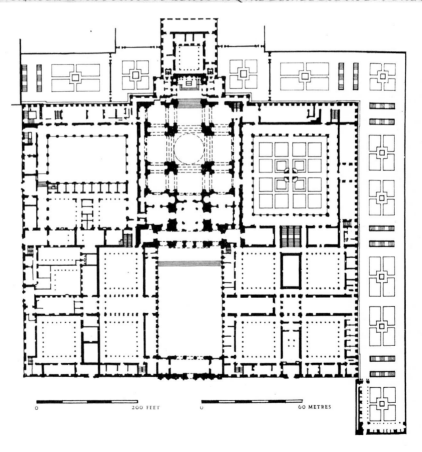

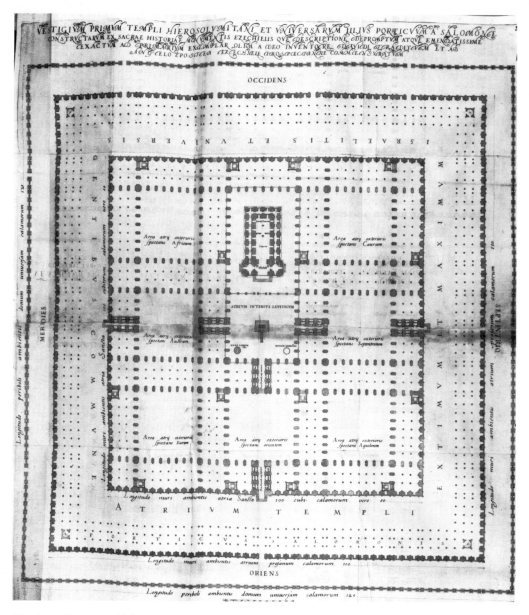

**99** Juan Bautista Villalpando, *In Ezechielem Explanationes,* ground plan of Temple Precincts (London, British Library)

**100** Juan Bautista Villalpando, *In Ezechielem Explanationes,* Holy of Holies, with Seraphim-like beings (London, British Library)

115

**101** Jan Luyken, *Afbeeldingen* . . . , views of the Temple Precincts and interior (London, British Library)

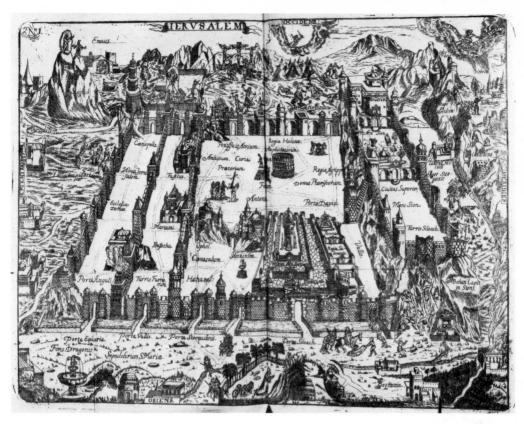

**102** Leonhard Rauwolf, *Itinerarium per Palaestinam,* folding map of Jerusalem showing Crucifixion (top centre) and Temptation of Christ (top right), similar to the latter episode's inclusion in Schedel's view of Jerusalem (ill. 56) (London, British Library)

**103**   Francesco Borromini, dome of Church of Sant' Ivo della Sapienza, Rome (photo, Alinari)

(*opposite top*)
**104**   Johann Bernhard Fischer von Erlach, *Entwürff* . . . (English edition of 1737), side view of Church of St. Charles Borromaeus, Vienna (London, British Library)

(*opposite bottom*)
**105**   Johann Bernhard Fischer von Erlach, view of Church of St. Charles Borromaeus, Vienna

AMSTELÆDAMI, Excudunt GERARDUS & JACOBUS BORSTIUS cɪɔɪɔccɪɪ.

**106** G. Surenhusius, *Mischna,* views of Temple and Precincts as well as ritual scenes, signed C. Huyberts (London, British Library)

AMSTELÆDAMI, Excudunt GERARDUS & JACOBUS BORSTIUS cIↃ IↃ CLXXXXVIIII.

**107**  G. Surenhusius, *Mischna,* view of Temple Precincts with other festive scenes (London, British Library)

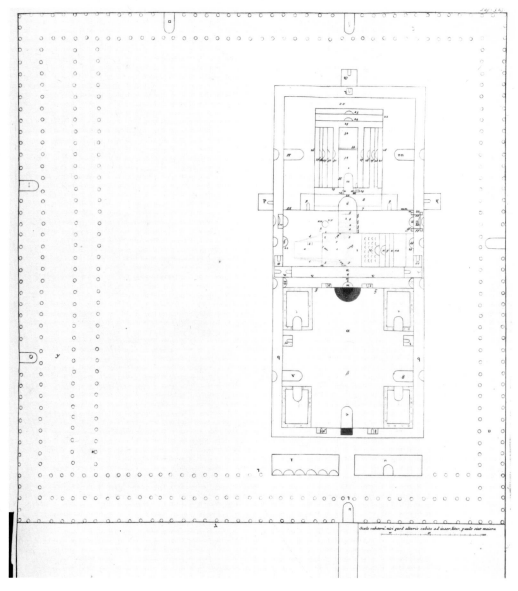

**108** Constantin L'Empereur, from Surenhusius's *Mischnah,* ground plan of the Temple (London, British Library)

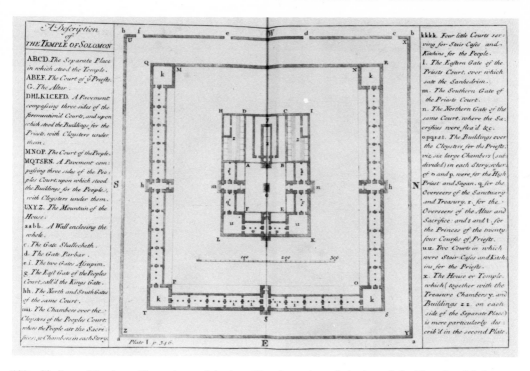

**109** Sir Isaac Newton, *Chronology of Ancient Kingdoms Amended*, plan of the Temple of Solomon
(London, British Library)

**110** Bernard Lamy, *De Tabernaculo* . . . , substructure of platform of Solomon's Temple (London, British Library)

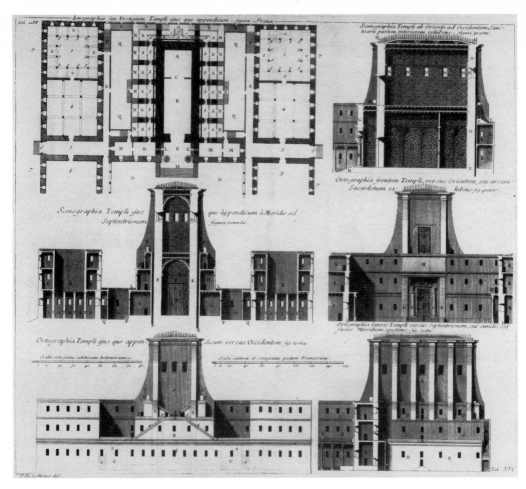

**111** Bernard Lamy, *De Tabernaculo* . . . , elevations and ground plan of Solomon's Temple (London, British Library)

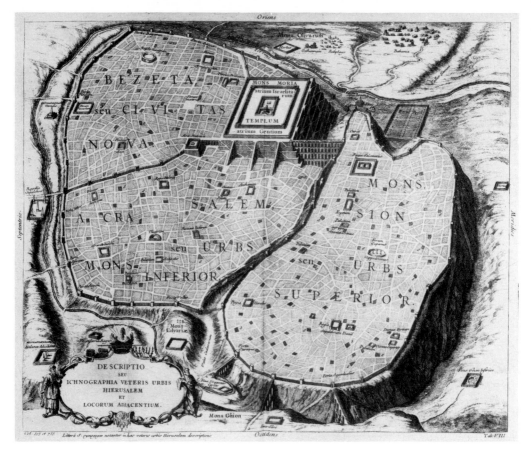

**112**  Bernard Lamy, *De Tabernaculo . . .* , map of Jerusalem (London, British Library)

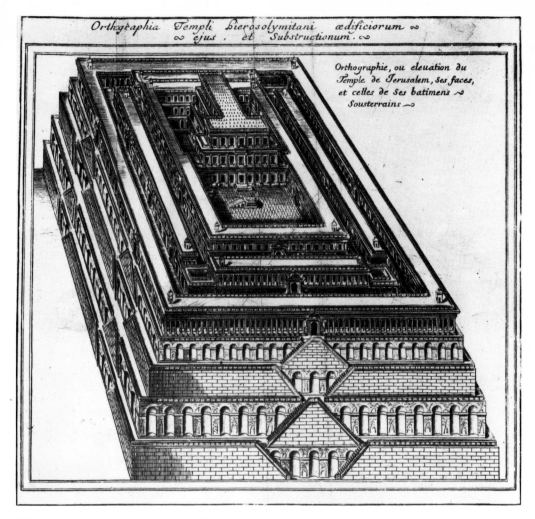

**113** Bernard Lamy, *Introduction à l'écriture sainte,* substructure of platform of Solomon's Temple (London, British Library)

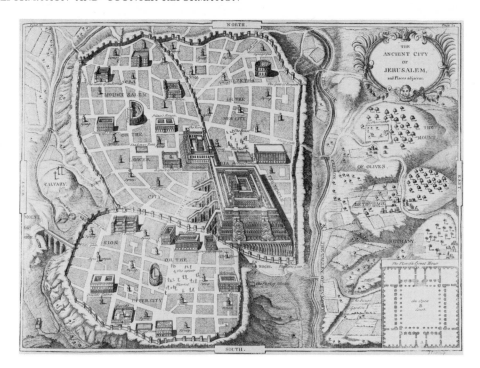

The Great SANHEDRIM.

**116**  Louis Maillet, *Les figures du Temple et du palais de Salomon,* tower of Solomon's Temple (Paris, Bibliothèque Nationale)

(*opposite top*)
**114**  Richard Bundy, *Apparatus Biblicus* . . . , map of Jerusalem (London, British Library)

(*opposite bottom*)
**115**  Richard Bundy, *Apparatus Biblicus* . . . , exedra of the Sanhedrin or judicial council, derived from Lamy (London, British Library)

**117** Louis Maillet, *Les figures du Temple et du palais de Salomon,* section of tower of Solomon's Temple (Paris, Bibliothèque Nationale)

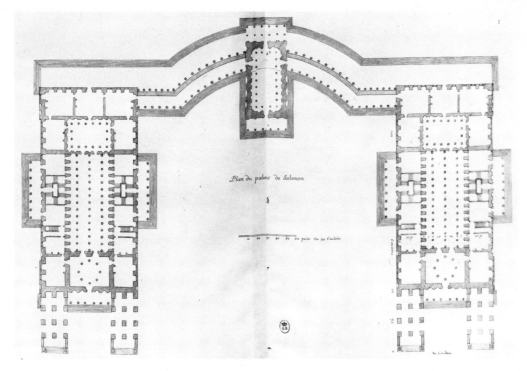

**118**  Louis Maillet, *Les figures du Temple et du palais de Salomon,* ground plan of Solomon's palace (Paris, Bibliothèque Nationale)

**119**  Louis Maillet, *Les figures du Temple et du palais de Salomon,* view of Solomon's palace (Paris, Bibliothèque Nationale)

131

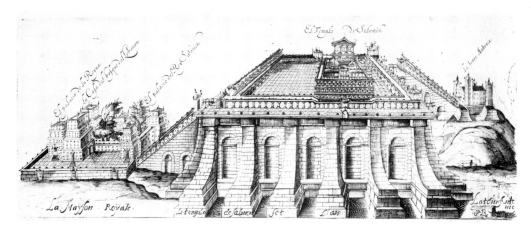

**120**   Jacob Judah Leon, *Retrato del Templo de Selomoh,* view of Solomon's Temple, his palace and the Fortress Antonia (London, British Library)

**121**   Jacob Judah Leon, *Afbeeldinghe van den Tempel Salomonis,* view of Solomon's Temple, his palace and the Fortress Antonia (London, British Library)

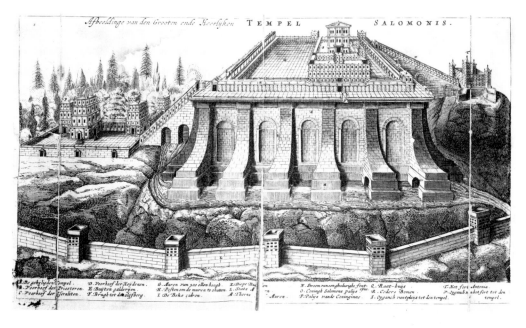

CHAPTER V

# Contributions to the Baroque and the Enlightenment

UP TO THIS point in time the lives of Jewish craftsmen and artists remained in the shadow. It is, therefore, particularly interesting that in the seventeenth century we encounter a rabbi who was also a craftsman and a model-builder, Jacob Judah (Aryeh) Leon (c. 1603–1675). This is all the more remarkable because models generally dealt with contemporary buildings, being either popular in order to assist patrons to make their choices or valued as mementoes of important buildings, and Jacob Judah (Aryeh) Leon appears to have been the first Jew to build models for historical considerations.

A Sephardi, he became so famous through his Temple model of 1641 that he acquired the surname 'Templo'. Although Templo was not a profound thinker and only a minor character in the process of history, his architectural interests and international connections are worth studying. He was ambitious and successful as an architectural expert, and this is demonstrated by the 'privileges' of the States General and of the States of Holland and Zeeland which he obtained for the Spanish and Dutch editions of his book on the Temple, *Retrato del Templo de Selomoh* and *Afbeeldinghe van den Tempel Salomonis* (1642, Middelburg and Amsterdam respectively). These privileges were repeated for the French edition of 1643, *Portraict du Temple de Salomon*, published in Amsterdam. He was supposed to have been a Freemason, and although this was not impossible for a Jew in England, there is no evidence to support the suggestion. However, a Jewish influence on Freemasons in general is certain.[1]

As usual in the Middle Ages and during Templo's own period, a height of 120 cubits for the porch was accepted, following II *Chronicles* 3: 4. I *Kings* 6:2, 3 give no height for the porch but cite thirty cubits for the Temple as a whole. This particular problem did not worry Templo, who ignored it, in contrast to Villalpando, who had suggested a façade of three storeys, thus accommodating both measurements, a solution reminiscent of the commentaries of Rashi and Kimche on *Chronicles*, which apply measurements as specified in *Chronicles* to the whole façade,

*ILL. 120*
*ILL. 121*

*p. 185*
*p. 184*

133

while allocating the one in *Kings* only to the ground floor. Josephus also had accepted the full height of the Temple façade as did Agrippa (*The Jewish War, op. cit.*, pp. 392 and 266).

An engraving in Templo's *Retrato* is meant to represent the Temple,   *ILL. 120* together with the palace of Solomon and the Fortress Antonia. The Temple is placed asymmetrically, according to Jewish tradition, perhaps indebted to the plan published in 1630 by Constantin L'Empereur (1591–1648).[2] L'Empereur was a famous Christian Talmudist, whose design for the ground plan was published in Surenhusius's *Mischna* (see p. 96). The captions are in two different languages and the French ones, set out professionally, read, *La Mayson Royale, Le Temple de Salomon, Fet L'An 1642, La Tour Antonie*, with the initials P.B. The longer text is in Spanish, written in a thinner script and, no doubt, suggested by Templo. Although the identity of 'P.B.' cannot be more closely established, he was a man of considerable skill, perhaps a French Huguenot who had found refuge in Holland. Particularly interesting is his vision, in an austere Mannerist style, of the palatial precincts, not unlike the compositions of Jacques Perret. The wind-swept trees appear out of proportion and, for   *ILL. 88* this very reason, they are aesthetically effective. The spelling of *mayson* is rather unusual and may indicate the engraver's origin in the south of France. The same engraving is used on a broadsheet of c. 1642 advertising Templo's work, without the French text and signature. In eliminating the engraver's identity and leaving blank spaces, especially at the base of the buttresses, Templo was not transgressing the code of behaviour of his time for in the seventeenth century the use of suitable material without acknowledgement was not considered to be plagiarism but, rather, was normal practice. In a similar engraving of a later edition of the *Retrato*, the Spanish captions were, in their turn, eliminated to be replaced by Dutch ones, again, presumably, composed by Templo. This design, which became very popular, is of much coarser quality and it is found in numerous examples in the Bibliotheca Rosenthaliana, Amsterdam. It was used in   *ILL. 121* J. Saubert's Latin translation *Jacobi Jehudae Leonis de Templo Hierosolomytano*, published in Helmsted in 1665 and influencing Caramuel von Lobkowitz's Temple engraving in *Architectura Civil Recta y Obliqua* of   *ILL. 122* 1678. The design in the latter is simplified considerably, the decorative trees from the Templo engravings replaced by a forest in the background, based on *Ezekiel* 17: 22, and the 'waters' added, according to *Ezekiel* 47: 1.[3] Caramuel also included a view of the Escorial in his treatise.   *ILL. 123*

Templo's intriguing figure reveals him as an enlightened author of illustrated books, drawing on biblical, talmudic and later rabbinic sources. Just as he was no architect, a term loosely used in the eighteenth century and applied incorrectly to him by M. P. Decastro, perhaps a descendant,

neither was he an engraver. He was, however, an innovator in the field of
*ILL. 124* book illustration and iconography relating to the Temple and the Tabernacle and opened the eyes of the Jewish and also, to a large degree, of the Christian reading public to the value of Jewish tradition in architectural thought, as reflected in engravings. In addition, Templo produced two models, the first being of the Temple and the later one of the Tabernacle, which were much admired and made a greater impact than pictures or prints could have achieved. Unfortunately both of these models have been destroyed, although one of them, the Temple model, belonged to M. P. Decastro in 1778 and had probably been brought to England by Templo himself, as a letter of introduction dated 1670 from Christian Huygens to Sir Christopher Wren suggests.[4] Templo's Temple model understandably influenced the architecture of the Portuguese Synagogue built between 1670 and 1675 in Amsterdam. This is particularly clear in the shape of the buttresses, based originally on Villalpando's illustrations but inspired by this model.

Another notable model, of later date, was made by a German Christian,
*ILLS. 125, 126* Gerhard Schott, and is now preserved in the Museum für Hamburgische Geschichte. Constructed of timber, Schott's model shows clearly the various courts and elevations, while omitting the palace of Solomon and the Fortress Antonia, clearly described in Templo's engravings and presumably part of the latter's model. Schott's model was completed in 1694 and slavishly copies the plates of Villalpando's volume, showing none of the personal choice and unconventional adaptations typical of Templo.[5]

The famous and much copied Amsterdam edition of the Haggadah, the ritual for Passover, of 1695 was the work of a convert to Judaism,
*ILL. 127* Abraham ben Jacob, 'Abraham' being the usual adopted name of a proselyte. He was a former preacher who introduced many new elements into the illustrations, among them the Temple picture derived from the
*ILL. 128* *Icones Bibliae* by Matthaeus Merian the elder. Abraham ben Jacob widened the scope of Jewish book illustration by introducing skills acquired from non-Jews.[6] The two free-standing columns in the *Icones Bibliae* may have been derived from Vatablus's Bible which led Abraham ben Jacob to fuse Villalpando's reconstruction of Ezekiel's Temple with Merian's prototype. This synthesis should have appealed to Abraham ben Jacob, as it asserts the unity of the Temple vision. It should be remembered that Merian used a wide variety of prototypes, including
*ILL. 129* Gothic churches, as seen in the depiction of Solomon kneeling in the Temple.

Claude Perrault's Temple reconstruction has been mentioned (p. 92), but it is worth remembering that it was a baptized Jew, Louis Compiègne

de Veil, whose work inspired it. Veil, a scholar and translator of Maimonides, may have helped to achieve the architectural correctness that
surpassed the standards of his time.[7]

Rembrandt's deep involvement in Jewish matters has also been discussed
earlier. In his work, and in that of his school, the Temple appears as a
Baroque, central building, perhaps still retaining a reminiscence of the
Dome of the Rock. This is seen in a painting of c. 1650 in the Edinburgh
National Gallery (Duke of Sutherland loan) perhaps *Hannah Teaching*     *ILL. 130*
*Samuel*, and in *The Reconciliation of David and Absalom* of 1642 in
Leningrad, mentioned on page 68. If these interpretations are correct,
then the Temple is established symbolically here, prior to its building
during Solomon's reign. The architecture of the Temple in *The Presenta-*
*tion of the Christ Child* of 1631 in the Mauritshuis at The Hague is of similar   *ILL. 131*
nature. Surprisingly, Rembrandt's influence on Jewish artists for a long
period was negligible, and his importance for pictorial interpretation of
Jews was 're-evaluated' only in the nineteenth century by Joseph Israels
and Max Liebermann.[8]

The concept of the Temple made a strong impact on Hebrew book
decoration, not only in mediaeval manuscripts but also on woodcuts
and engravings. This tradition influenced folk art, especially that of the
eighteenth century, as exemplified by Eliezer Sussmann in the Synagogues
of Horb, Schwäbisch-Hall, Bechhofen and Kirchheim (see page 66).     *ILLS. 63, 64, 65*
Sussmann found his inspiration in the image of Jerusalem and expressed
himself also in a figurative style and floral motifs. To the same group
belongs the folding *sukkah* from Fischach now in the Israel Museum,
Jerusalem, which, although dating from the early nineteenth century,
still relates to the earlier pictorial tradition. It also influenced topographical representations in Jewish folk art.[9]     *ILLS. 66, 67*

It has to be remembered that in the late eighteenth century the Jews
were dispersed throughout Europe and struggled for religious tolerance
and civic emancipation. These ideals had been widely advocated, notably
by Moses Mendelssohn, the Jewish philosopher, in Germany and by the
Abbé Grégoire in France. The French Revolution espoused the cause of
liberty whilst, at the same time, distrusting religious activities and,
although Napoleon initially favoured progressive forces and proclaimed
edicts that were of advantage to Jewish individuals and Sephardic communities, these were of doubtful value to the Ashkenazic communities,
especially those in Alsace. Nonetheless, the *Code Napoléon* meant liberty
for the majority of Jews, more particularly in the kingdom of Westphalia
under Jerome, Napoleon's brother, where emancipation became a reality.
It is also a period in which individual Jews in France, or under French
influence, were reluctantly admitted as Freemasons. (It hardly needs to

*ILL. 84*    be said that the Temple and its ritual influenced Freemasons.[10])

The Rhineland was occupied by French Revolutionary troops and the grand duchy of Baden was established by Napoleon, who also incorporated Brunswick into Westphalia between 1807 and 1813. However, the influence of the Berlin salons and their fashionable society in the direction of emancipation had preceded the legal innovations both of the Emperor Joseph II in Austria and of the French Revolution, and in Germany Christian Wilhelm Dohm propagated the ideas of the Enlightenment and the 'betterment' of the Jews, morally as well as socially, as early as 1781 in his *Geschichte des Jüdischen Volkes*.[11]

By a historical paradox the Temple ideal, nurtured by Calvinist habits, was revived from the past and led to the designation of contemporary Jewish houses of worship as 'temples'. Duke Charles William Ferdinand of Brunswick (1760–1806), the benefactor of Israel Jacobson, who served the duke as court Jew, corresponded with Moses Mendelssohn and abrogated the body tax levied on Jews. Israel Jacobson himself founded a
*ILL. 132*    school in Seesen in 1801 and also founded there in 1810 the Jacobstempel, the synagogue dedicated to the memory of his father Jacob.[12] Israel Jacobson regarded this building as a 'humble copy' of the Temple in Jerusalem, the allusion here being based more on spiritual renewal than on any architectural model. Later, in 1818, a Reform temple was erected in Hamburg. Ideologically, the Jews had discovered a contemporary meaning in the concept of the Temple and expressed it in synagogue building. They became active patrons of architecture. Two synagogues are of special interest in this context, one planned by a Catholic architect and the other by a Protestant. The first of these was designed between 1787 and 1789 by Peter Krahe and erected in Düsseldorf, while the other, by Friedrich Weinbrenner, was built in Karlsruhe in 1798.[13]

Peter Krahe's tripartite precincts consisted of an entrance portion
*ILL. 134*    containing both the rabbi's and the precentor's residences, followed by a
*ILL. 133*    semi-circular forecourt, later to be changed into a rectangular one by Peter Koehler in 1802, while the layout culminated in the synagogue proper with its women's galleries. The whole scheme recalls the idea of the Temple standing within and at the rear of its courts. The architectural elements, based on French Neo-Classicism, were characterized by austere and simplified forms. This synagogue was replaced by a larger one after its demolition in 1873. The house for the rabbi and the precentor within the precincts of the synagogue is particularly interesting for its compactness. The arrangements for internal circulation are similar to those of the Paris mansions of the late eighteenth century, providing a variety of rooms in a restricted space and, frequently, accompanied by a semi-circular court. The influence of Ledoux and his contemporaries is strongly seen, especially

137

in the elevations.[14] This influence presents no chronological difficulty, as the famous toll pavilions by Ledoux, the so-called 'propylées', had been erected between 1784 and 1789. Furthermore, French topographical engravings were accessible all over Europe, especially popular prints and the collection of prize designs of the French Académie.[15]

Although Krahe seems not to have visited France, he was in the Rhineland, near to what was then regarded as the centre of civilization. The evidence of French influence in his design for the synagogue at Düsseldorf is, therefore, only to be expected. The compact arrangement of the floor plan shows the ritual bath on the right, marked 'D', and *ILL. 134* next to it, marked 'F', is the entrance to the women's gallery. The ambulatory, surrounding the synagogue proper, made provision for ritual processions, whilst the house for the rabbi and the precentor was divided into two independent units that were accessible by separate staircases, *ILL. 133* marked 'K' and 'F' respectively.

Even more significant was the Temple influence on Weinbrenner's Karlsruhe synagogue in 1798. Weinbrenner was an outstandingly thoughtful architect who consciously attempted an oriental style by introducing two pylon-like columns, reminiscent of the columns Jachin and Boaz. *ILL. 135* The division of the precinct into entrance towers, forecourt and synagogue proper clearly reveals the Temple influence, a type of planning with a forecourt which still persists in the twentieth century. The structure with its women's galleries, although made of timber, nevertheless, had a *ILLS. 136, 137* monumental character. Unfortunately, it was destroyed by fire in 1871. Although the Jews had acquired the site at an earlier date, it is particularly interesting to see how Weinbrenner's synagogue fits into the expanded town of Karlsruhe as depicted in Weinbrenner's own plan of 1822.[16]

In France the term 'temple' had been popularized for places of worship, first by the Protestants and later for churches in general. It was also applied to synagogues. The Synagogue of Bordeaux, built by Arnaud Corcelles in 1812 and destroyed by fire in 1873, was set within the same tradition. The building was placed in a forecourt and had a Neo-Classical portico adorned by two columns, once again motivated, perhaps, by the *ILL. 138* familiar tradition of Jachin and Boaz in the description of Solomon's Temple. The interior took the form of a basilica with galleries for women *ILL. 139* and was covered by a timber roof, as in the case of the still extant Protestant 'temple' by the same architect, completed in 1835.[17]

The most outstanding example of a synagogue standing for the Temple was, perhaps, the Temple of the Rue Notre-Dame-de-Nazareth, Paris, built by the Belgian P. J. Sandrié and Jacob Silveyra of Bordeaux, the latter being probably of Sephardi extraction. The building was completed in 1822 but was closed in 1850. It had an inner Doric order supporting

*ILL. 141*  the women's gallery and a façade of a simple form in the forecourt, the layout again evoking the Temple tradition. It is significant that its dedication was modern and traditional at the same time, the inscriptions
*ILL. 140*  stating 'Temple Israélite de Paris 1822' on the architrave and 'Beth Adonai' over the main door; the latter, no doubt, led to the men's part of the synagogue while the side doors connected with the women's galleries. It is for this synagogue that Gottfried Semper initially created his monu-
*ILL. 148*  mental design of 1850, which unfortunately was not executed.[18] Before the bombing raids on London during the 1939–45 war there were similar
*ILL. 142*  galleries to be seen at the Neo-Classical Great Synagogue, designed by James Spiller, a pupil of James Wyatt, and built from 1788 to 1790, which presented a fine example in the style of the Adam brothers, typical of the period.[19]

A synagogue in a severely classical mode was erected in Budapest by A. Landesherr as late as 1920–21. It was conceived as a temple in the Graeco-Roman manner. It should here be remembered that a Hungarian place of worship, whether Jewish or Christian, was and is still called a 'templom', and this fact may help to suggest Classical revival. The type of façade found in Budapest is not exceptional, an outstanding example being
*ILL. 143*  the Beth-Elohim Synagogue in Charleston built by a Jewish architect, David Lopez, in 1841.[20]

Unfortunately, most of the buildings mentioned here were destroyed later in the nineteenth century in order to give more space for enlarged Jewish congregations. Among these was the Munich synagogue built by a French Catholic architect, Jean-Baptiste Métivier, who was certainly not a Huguenot as suggested by Rachel Wischnitzer. The synagogue, built in 1824–25, was consecrated in 1826. It was erected in the Neo-Classical tradition in the form of a Roman basilica and showed the distinction that is characteristic of Métivier's work for the Bavarian court, a testimony to the social standing of the Jewish community.[21]

When Gothic became the prevalent church style, it was also adopted for synagogues, although the designation of 'temple' was retained. This is clearly exemplified by the New Israelitic Temple of Hamburg,
*ILL. 144*  built by J. H. Klees-Wuelbern in 1842–44. The façade was adorned by two small Neo-Gothic turrets and this pattern was repeated in synagogues in Budapest, Berlin and many other places.[22]

The influence of the Temple tradition clearly persisted in the sense of longitudinal direction towards the sanctuary in Neo-Classical synagogues[23] and certain architectural details based on scripture were maintained, such as the forecourts, the free-standing columns and the unadorned façades. The main post-mediaeval tradition was the inclusion of women's galleries, which had been popular in synagogues for centuries but can only in the vaguest of ways be connected with the women's courts and galleries surrounding the Temple. They have to be recognized as an innovation that ultimately connects with the Graeco-Roman synagogue, thus affording an element of continuity, coupled with functional change.

An interesting sidelight on the degree of toleration and concern for Jewish values in England is found in a work published in Bath in 1741 by the architect John Wood the elder (1704–1754), the title of which speaks for itself, *The Origin of Building or the Plagiarism of the Heathens Detected.* Wisely, John Wood included few elevations in his plates and those mostly of details. He showed mainly ground plans, among them those of the Tabernacle (pls. 2, 3), the Temple óf Solomon (pls. 24, 25), Ezekiel's *ILL. 146* vision (pls. 27–30) and Solomon's palace (pl. 26). The view of John Wood *ILL. 147* is that Vitruvius and the ancients derived their style from Jewish art, a claim based on the search to find primitive sources for European *ILL. 145* developments. It is the same concern that inspired his *Study of Stonehenge*, published in 1747. In this respect he ascribed more to Jewish example than Jews themselves would have been prepared to claim, and this may well have been based upon the influence of Freemasons who, in turn, were influenced by the pictorial tradition of the Temple.[24]

The acceptance of the Jewish communities, as opposed to mere toleration, is a problem that had so far not arisen. Jews were still regarded as outsiders, even by such broad-minded spirits as Goethe, but during the period of Emancipation and Enlightenment public attitudes were changing, among Christians as well as among Jews. The latter insisted on being regarded as citizens of their respective countries, sharing burdens as well as privileges, and in this they had the support of Christian sympathizers. Their attitude, nevertheless, engendered resistance among the more conservative Jewish believers and created problems which, however, failed to affect architecture. Neo-Classicism was the ruling fashion, and this affected synagogue art, whether designed to serve conservative or reformist Jewry. The divergence between them influenced types of worship but did not sway taste, whether in the more emancipated temple or the more traditional *shul*.

### References

1  H. Rosenau in *Journal of Jewish Studies*, vol. XXIII (1972), pp. 72 ff. See also *De Tempel van Salomo* (The Hague 1976), *passim*. For background O. S. Rankin, *Jewish Religious Polemic* (Edinburgh 1956), pp. 89 ff.; L. Dermott, *Ahiman Rezon*, especially edition of 1776; W. J. Chetwolde Crawley in *Transactions of the Quatuor Coronati Lodge*, vol. XII (1899), pp. 150 ff. R. Le Forestier, *La Franc-Maçonnerie templière et occultiste aux XVIII et XIX Siècles* (Paris and Louvain 1970), *passim*.

2   C. L'Empereur, *Talmudis Babylonici Codex Middoth* etc. (Leiden 1630).

3   Templo influenced J. Caramuel von Lobkowitz's Temple picture in *Architectura Civil Recta y Obliqua* (Vigeven 1678), part 9, lamina A. The relationship between Caramuel and Templo had already been noted by Herrmann, *op. cit.* On the other hand, R. Taylor in *Academia*, vol. II (1952), pp. 13 ff., esp. p. 49, fails to realize the connection between the two engravings.

4   First published in J. A. Worp, *Briefwisseling*, vol. VI (*Rijks Geschiedkundige Publicatien*, no. 32) (1917), pp. 274–75. The letter to Wren reads: 'This bearer is a Jew by birth and profession, and I am bound to him for some instruction I had from him, long agoe, in the Hebrew literature. This maketh me grant him the addresses he desireth of me, his intention being to shew in England a curious model of the Temple of Salomon, he hath been about to contrive these many years, where he doth presume to have demonstrated and corrected an infinite number of errors and paralogismes of our most learned schollars, who have meddled with the exposition of that holy fabrick, and most specially of the Jesuit Villalpandus, who, as you know, Sir, has handled the matter "ingenti cum fastu et apparatu, ut solent isti".' See Stephen Wren, *Parentalia* (London 1750), pp. 59 and 351 ff. I am indebted to Mr. H. J. Louw for the Huygens reference.

5   On the so-called Schott model see K. V. Riedel in *Beiträge zur Deutschen Volks- und Altertumskunde*, vol. XI (1967), pp. 117 ff. Cf. *Jahresbericht des Museums für Hamburgische Geschichte*, vol. 4, beiheft I (1911), pp. 17 ff. and *The Temple of Solomon* etc. (London 1725). This anonymous book was kindly made available to me by Mr. P. Breman.

6   R. Wischnitzer-Bernstein in *Monatsschrift für Geschichte und Wissenschaft des Judentums,* vol. XXXIX (1931), pp. 269 ff.

7   Herrmann, *op. cit., passim.*

8   A. Bredius, *Rembrandt*, especially Bredius no. 511, *The Reconciliation of David and Absalom* of 1642 in Leningrad. The interpretation of the theme as David and Jonathan is unlikely because of the contrast in age between the two male protagonists. See F. Landsberger, *Rembrandt, the Jews and the Bible* (Philadelphia 1946), pp. 145 ff. It is interesting in this context that Rembrandt's *Jewish Bride*, the subject matter of which is sometimes disputed, shows a couple in an open courtyard, a fact which only became clear after the cleaning of the painting. It was a Jewish custom to hold weddings in the open courtyards of synagogues in the past. The ceremony is now usually conducted inside the synagogues. See the article on 'marriage' in *Encyclopaedia Judaica*.

9   *Monumenta Judaica, Katalog* (Cologne 1963), E. 259 and 260; B. Narkiss (ed.), *Picture History of Jewish Civilization* (New York 1970), p. 188; D. Davidovicz, *Wandmalereien in alten Synagogen: Das Wirken des Malers Elieser Sussmann in Deutschland* (Hameln and Hamburg 1969); Z. Wilbusch in *The Israel Museum News*, vol. X (1975), pp. 100 ff.

10  R. Anschel, *Napoléon et les Juifs* (Paris 1928); A. Lantoine, *Histoire de la Franc-Maçonnerie Française* (Paris 1925), pp. 22 ff.; A. Hertzberg, *The French Enlighten-ment and the Jews* (New York and London 1968); J. Katz, *Jews and Freemasons in Europe, 1723–1932* (Cambridge, Massachusetts 1970); S. M. Dubnow, *op. cit.*; *Monumenta Judaica, Handbuch, passim*; F. Kobler, *Napoleon and the Jews* (New York 1976). See also note 1 above.

11  A. Altmann in *Leo Baeck Yearbook,* vol. VI (1961), pp. 3 ff. The best book on German synagogues during the Emancipation is H. Hammer-Schenk, *Unter-*

*suchungen zum Synagogenbau in Deutschland* (Tübingen diss, Bamberg 1974).

12  On Jacobson cf. Wischnitzer, *The European Synagogue*, pp. 174 ff.; also A. Geiger, *Judaism and its History* (New York 1866); Baron (1st edn.), vol. II, pp. 201 ff.; G. Ballin, 'Die Jacobsschule in Seesen', *1000 Jahre Seesen* (Seesen 1974).

13  The most important sources for the study of the Düsseldorf synagogue plans are found in R. Klaphek's contribution to *Wasmuths Monatshefte*, vol. IV (1919–20), pp. 253 ff. His research is reflected by E. Moses in *Aus der Geschichte der Juden im Rheinland, Jüdische Kult- und Kunstdenkmäler,* published by the Rheinischer Verein für Denkmalspflege und Heimatschutz (1951), heft I, pp. 122 ff. R. Dorn, *Peter Krahe* (Brunswick 1969–71), vol. II, pp. 44 ff. and *passim*, has little to contribute to the subject of Jewish art, but has to be challenged with regard to French influence, which he denies. H. Rosenau in *Leo Baeck Yearbook*, vol. VIII (1963), pp. 214 ff.

14  H. Rosenau, *Social Purpose in Architecture* (London 1970), *passim*; L. Hautecoeur, *Histoire de l'architecture classique en France* (Paris 1943–57), vol. IV, *passim*, especially pp. 380 and 385 on staircases, curved courtyards and balconies. M. Gallet, *Paris Domestic Architecture of the 18th Century* (London 1972).

15  H. Rosenau in *Architectural History*, vol. III (1960), *passim*.

16  A. Valdenaire, *F. Weinbrenner* (Karlsruhe 1919), pp. 59, 60, 64; K. Ehrenberg, *Baugeschichte von Karlsruhe* (Karlsruhe 1908), *passim*; H. Rosenau in *Leo Baeck Yearbook*, vol. VIII (1963), pp. 217 ff. On the Egyptian derivation cf. A. Hirst, *Der Tempel Salomonis* (Berlin 1809), based on a lecture delivered in 1804.

17  The original watercolours by Auguste Bordes are now owned by the Société Archéologique de Bordeaux, but preserved in the Archives Municipales of Bordeaux. I wish to express my gratitude to Professor F.-G. Pariset and M. J. P. Avisseau, the Municipal Archivist, for a pleasant and instructive visit. On Bordeaux, see L. Desgraves in F.-G. Pariset (ed.), *Histoire de Bordeaux*, vol. 5: *Bordeaux au XVIII<sup>e</sup> siècle* (Bordeaux 1968), *passim*, esp. pp. 150 ff.; also J. Cohen, *Journal d'un Rabbin* (Bordeaux 1969). Cf. J.-F. Mouilleseaux, catalogue of the exhibition *Les architectes Bordelais et le Néo-Classicisme* (Bordeaux 1970). The synagogue was rebuilt on a different site by Charles Durand and completed in 1882.

18  Sandrié was also the architect of the Church of Notre-Dame-de-Lorette in Paris. Thieme-Becker with good bibliography on Sandrié; Wischnitzer, *The European Synagogue*, p. 173. H. Rosenau in *Leo Baeck Yearbook*, vol. VIII (1963), pp. 214 ff. and vol. XXII (1977), pp. 237 ff.

19  Rosenau, *Jewish Art*, pp. 38 ff.

20  E. Jamilly in *Jewish Art, an Illustrated History* (ed. C. Roth) (London 1961), figs. 358 and 359.

21  Cf. H. Rose-Jena in *Zeitschrift des Vereins für Kunstwissenschaft,* vol. 1 (1934), pp. 49 ff.

22  On J. H. Klees-Wuelbern cf. Thieme-Becker and *Der Fremde in Hamburg* (Hamburg 1846).

23  *Middoth, passim*. See chapter I of this study.

24  F. A. Yates, *The Rosicrucian Enlightenment* (London 1972), p. 213. See note 1 of this chapter.

**122**  Caramuel von Lobkowitz, *Architectura Civil Recta y Obliqua*, Temple reconstruction based on that of Jacob Judah Leon (London, British Library)

**123**  Caramuel von Lobkowitz, *Architectura Civil Recta y Obliqua*, view of the Escorial (London, British Library)

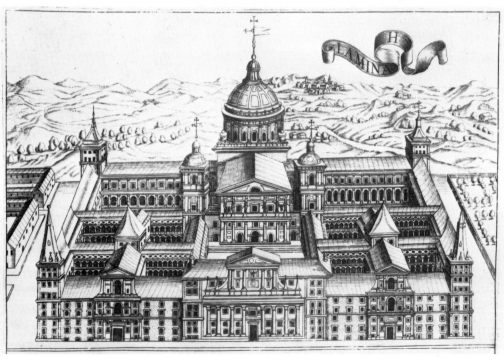

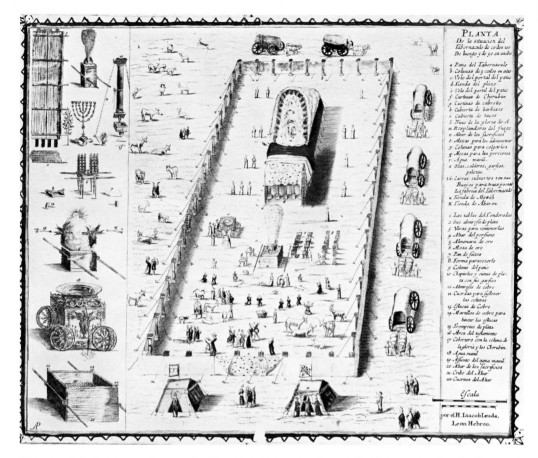

**124** Jacob Judah Leon, *Retrato del Templo de Selomoh,* view of the Tabernacle, ritual objects and wagons of the Israelites (London, British Library)

**125**  Gerhard Schott,
model of the Temple (Hamburg, Museum für Hamburgische Geschichte)

**126**  Gerhard Schott, model of the Temple
(Hamburg, Museum für Hamburgische
Geschichte)

**127** Abraham ben Jacob, Amsterdam Haggadah, view of Solomon's Temple Precincts in Jerusalem

(*opposite top*)
**128** Matthaeus Merian the elder, *Icones Bibliae,* view of Solomon's Temple Precincts in Jerusalem (London, British Library)

(*opposite bottom*)
**129** Matthaeus Merian the elder, *Icones Bibliae,* King Solomon praying in the Temple (London, British Library)

147

**130** Rembrandt, *Hannah Teaching Samuel* (Edinburgh, National Gallery of Scotland, Duke of Sutherland loan)

**131**  Rembrandt, *Presentation of the Christ Child* (The Hague, Mauritshuis)

**132** Synagogue of the Jacobson School, known as the Jacobstempel, Seesen, from a photograph of 1901

(*bottom left*)
**133** Peter Krahe, Düsseldorf Synagogue and rabbi's and precentor's house, first-storey ground plan. The rabbi's part is marked 'G', the precentor's 'F'; the staircase marked 'E' leads to an upper floor for a school, a weekday synagogue and an infirmary. (Düsseldorf, Stadtgeschichtliches Museum)

(*bottom right*)
**134** Peter Krahe, Düsseldorf Synagogue and rabbi's and precentor's house, elevations (Düsseldorf, Stadtgeschichtliches Museum)

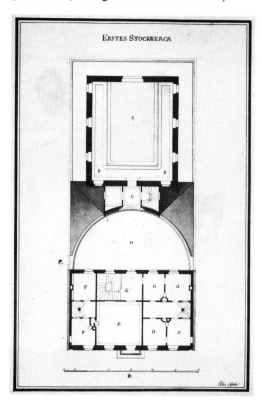

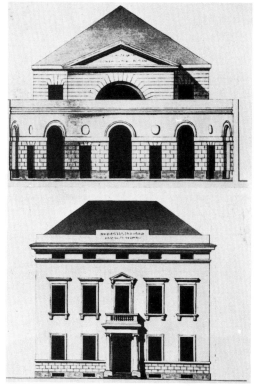

**135** Friedrich Weinbrenner, Karlsruhe
Synagogue, from P. Wagner

(*bottom left*)
**136** Johann Michael Voltz, Karlsruhe Synagogue, c. 1820 (Nördlingen, Stadtgeschichtliches
Museum)

(*bottom right*)
**137** Johann Michael Voltz, Karlsruhe Synagogue, interior, 1819 (Nördlingen, Stadtgeschichtliches
Museum)

138   Arnaud Corcelles, Synagogue of Bordeaux, exterior (Bordeaux, Archives Municipales)

(*opposite*)
139   Arnaud Corcelles, Synagogue of Bordeaux, interior (Bordeaux, Archives Municipales)

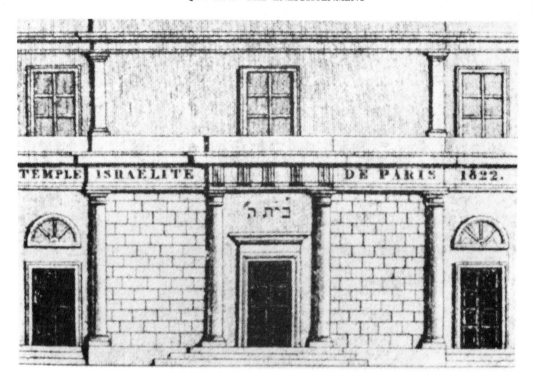

142   Augustus Welby Pugin, engraving of Great Synagogue, London, built by James Spiller, now destroyed

(*opposite top*)
140   P. J. Sandrié and Jacob Silveyra, Temple façade, Rue Notre-Dame-de-Nazareth, Paris, anonymous drawing

(*opposite bottom*)
141   P. J. Sandrié and Jacob Silveyra, Temple interior, Rue Notre-Dame-de-Nazareth, Paris, engraving of 1846

155

(*above left*)
**143** David Lopez, Beth-Elohim Synagogue, Charleston, South Carolina, an outstanding example of Doric revival

(*above right*)
**144** J. H. Klees-Wuelbern, New Israelitic Temple, Poolstrasse, Hamburg, 1842–44 (photo, Andres)

(*opposite*)
**145** John Wood the elder, sample page of *The Origin of Building,* relating Vitruvius's text to the biblical account (London, British Library)

## Chap. I.  *Plagiarifm of the Heathens Detected.*  9

was four Cubits, or very near one Diameter of the Pillar : And thus *Order* was not only reduced to a certain *Proportion*, but all the *Orders* were brought to their Perfection after the Space of Four Hundred and Eighty-Six Years and a Half, from their firft Introduction into Edifices ; this being the exact Period between the Time in which *Mofes* built the *Tabernacle*, and the Completion of the *Temple* by King *Solomon.*

Thus far Sacred Hiftory on the Origin of Building, as well as on the Rife, Progrefs and Perfection of the *Orders* of *Architecture*. We will now fee how thefe two Accounts ftand when fairly ftated together.

*VITRUVIUS* tells us, That Men at firft were born in Woods and Caverns, like the Beafts, and lived therein on the Fruits of the Earth.

*MOSES* tells us, That after Goᴅ had created Man, he planted a Garden with many Trees in it, and therein placed him to drefs it and to keep it, giving him for his Suftenance every green Herb, and the Fruit of every Tree but that of the Knowledge of Good and Evil.

*VITRUVIUS* says, That an impetuous Wind happening to arife, it pufhed the Trees in a certain Wood with fuch Violence againft one another, that by their Friction they took Fire ; which drove Mankind out from amongft them : This caufed Men to affemble together, to live in the fame Place, and to make *Huts* to dwell in ; *fome with Leaves,* others with Branches of Trees and Pieces of Clay ; while fome dug Lodges in the Mountains.

*MOSES* fays, That Man having difobey'd Goᴅ's Commands, his Nature was inftantly chang'd ; as foon as he found it, *he covered himfelf with Leaves* ; and when he heard the Voice and Motion of his Maker, *i. e.* an impetuous Wind, attended with Thunder and Lightning, he hid himfelf under the Trees ; Goᴅ inftantly drove him out of the Garden of *Eden*, and placed Cherubims with flaming Swords at the Eaft End thereof, to prevent his Accefs to the Tree of Life, and thereby make his new State immortal. After this, when *Adam* had a Grandchild born, his Son *Cain*, who had taken up his Abode in Obfcurity in a ftrange Land, which he called *Nod*, in Allufion to his Vagabond State, began to build *Huts* for his Family to dwell together in one collected Body.

C

*VI-*

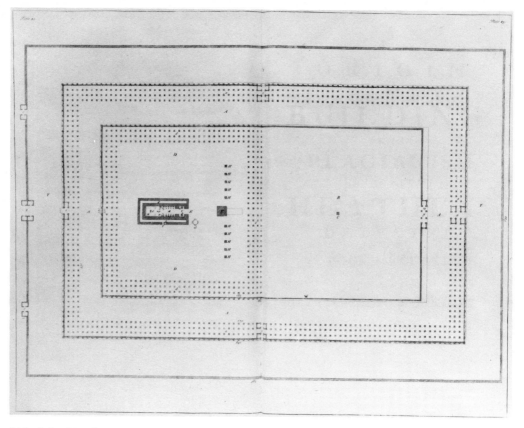

**146** John Wood the elder, *The Origin of Building,* engraving of ground plan of the Temple of Solomon (London, British Library)

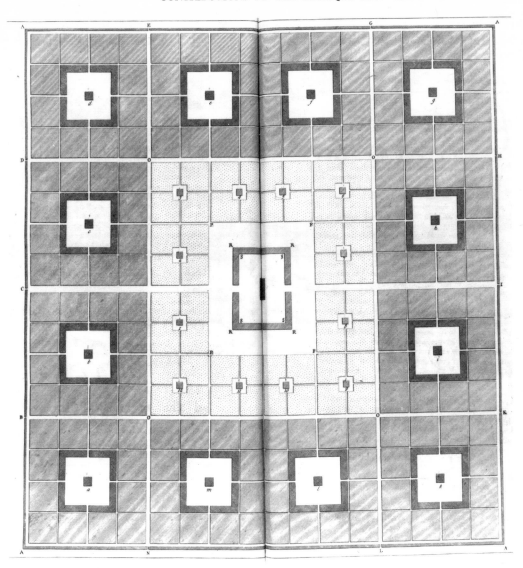

**147** John Wood the elder, *The Origin of Building,* engraving of ground plan of the Temple vision of Ezekiel (London, British Library)

**148** Gottfried Semper, design for the Temple of the Rue Notre-Dame-de-Nazareth, Paris, exterior view, 1850 (Zürich, Semper-Archiv)

CHAPTER VI

# Past Concepts
# and Future Trends

IN THE LATE nineteenth and the early twentieth centuries the long pent-up
creativity of the Jews in the visual arts suddenly flowered. This is true
of painting and sculpture as well as of architecture. The Jews concerned
were scarcely motivated by conscious religious interest. However, the ideas
expressed in the synagogue and the Temple are related to the sublime, as
has been previously suggested. This relationship did not result in slavish
copying of ancient models, but it could, on some occasions, provide
suggestions of an architectural nature as well as religious inspiration.

We have attempted to follow the evolution of the vision of the Temple
from its Hellenistic form through to the nineteenth century, and we now
have to consider the present period. Scientific investigation and archaeological exactitude are of major concern in Israel and, therefore, the
desire for correct reconstruction comes to the fore, although imaginative
and mystical symbolism is found in contemporary synagogues, some of
which are significantly connected with the Temple tradition. Among
contemporary painters Marc Chagall (b. 1887) is outstanding; his vision
of the Temple in the guise of the Dome of the Rock, particularly in
ILL. 149    *The Song of Songs*, a series of paintings in the Musée National Message
Biblique, Nice, mirrors the Holy City in a nostalgic mood.[1]

The ultimate in abstraction is found in Mark Rothko's Houghton
Chapel, where any denominational association is eschewed and a universal
attitude is attempted. The dedication took place in 1971, after the death
by suicide of the artist in 1970.[2]

The Marquis Charles Jean Melchior de Vogüé (1829–after 1909)
ILL. 150    emphasized the main structural features in his *Le Temple de Jérusalem*
(Paris 1864), whilst James Fergusson, the architect (1808–1864), in *The*
ILL. 151    *Temples of the Jews and Other Buildings* (London 1878) revealed a great
deal about oriental, even Indian, influences and Victorian taste, but
succeeded only in confusing the reader. Paradoxically, the more details
are given, the more the designs appear stylistically dated and misleading.
The reconstructions in *Die Stiftshütte, der Tempel in Jerusalem und der*

161

*Tempelplatz der Jetztzeit* (Berlin 1896) by C. Schick (1822–1901) are    *ILL. 152*
perhaps the most interesting of the group as he lived for many years in
Jerusalem and was an architect who closely studied Hebrew sources.
Obviously the object of this study is not archaeological detail, but the
quality of vision.

Gottfried Semper's (1803–1879) visionary and monumental but un-    *ILL. 148*
realized design for a Paris synagogue, the Temple of the Rue Notre-
Dame-de-Nazareth, which was to have been rebuilt on another site,
has been previously mentioned (see p. 139). It was an outstanding example
of stylistic historicism, the achievement of an artistic combination of older
forms, but by this approach producing a new, independent and authentic
work of art. Semper's definition of style, according to the appendix by
F. Pecht to *Der Stil* (Munich 1879), was 'Style is the accordance of an
art form with the history of its origin', thus making history part of the
artistic creation (vol. II, p. 572).

Semper's historicism can be compared with the theory of genetics,
according to which new organic forms emerge from earlier prototypes.
In this sense it is different from the mere copying from past forms and
embodies creative adaptations. It was in this spirit that Semper was one
of the first architects, if not the first, to enhance the exterior of synagogues
with the motif of the six-pointed star.[3]

It was Hegel, the great and too often neglected German philosopher,
who, perhaps, best expressed the characteristics of religious or, as he
called it, symbolic architecture.[4] It is the symbolic element which dis-
tinguishes architecture as an art from mere building for practical purposes,
and it is religion, understood in its widest sense, which provides the
impetus that generates artistic creation. As Hegel pointed out, there is in
religion a collective element, which is introverted and coupled with a
specific cult. For Judaism this vision was centred on the Temple which,
from the entrance right to the Holy of Holies, is clearly directional in
its emphasis. The Jewish paradox of a universal religion that, nevertheless,
is based on an earthly centre, can be understood literally or metaphorically.
In either case it reveals and perpetuates a sense of history, rooted in an
understanding of the sublime. It is for this reason that the tradition is
not handed down by highly individualized works such as Rembrandt's
paintings, but is related to lasting and typical elements, based on biblical
descriptions and measurements, the Temple façade being a case in point.

It is also characteristic that the proportions recorded for the length
of the Tabernacle and the Temple are simple. It will be remembered that
the length of the 'house' was forty cubits, directed towards the Holy of
Holies, which was a square of twenty cubits. These two structures can be
described as buildings consisting of a static rectangle and a square.

They are characterized by simplicity but also show a lack of flexibility that may amount to architectural monotony.[5] However, their simplicity of form is suitable for Jewish worship, emphasizing a sense of direction and allowing no distraction. Jewish architecture lacks the refinements associated with either Greek or Roman art and therefore precludes an attitude of 'art for art's sake'. It represents, instead, art for religion's sake, and it is only Villalpando and his followers who, in their Temple reconstructions, radically departed from this tradition by their emphasis on Vitruvius (see chapter III).

C. G. Jung in his numerous writings stressed the deep emotional appeal of the mandala, the square surrounded by, or including, a circle.[6] Directional buildings, as exemplified by the Tabernacle, the Jewish Temple and the church in the form of the basilica, have received less psychological attention; the possibility of their origins lying in Egyptian prototypes must remain a likely hypothesis.[7]

The idea of the Tabernacle as a universal sanctuary appeals to the modern mind. This tent does not stand initially for universality, because the structure itself is regarded as the numinous receptacle. Rather it is the idea of the Temple which, although originally connected with a sacred site, is transformed into a universal symbol, transcending time and space. This view is not accepted by a minority of Jews who take the injunction of rebuilding the Temple literally; it is coupled for them with the belief that the Messianic age will engender universal peace and brotherhood. Christians interpreted the Temple as an archetypal forerunner of the church, while the Jews, having regard to God's prohibition of its being built by David, who had sinned, saw it as a realization of the ideal of ethical purity (II *Samuel* 7: 5–12, I *Chronicles* 17: 4, 11; 28: 3). It is, therefore, not an ill-founded notion but a sign of spiritual continuity that the reformers of Christianity and of Judaism both set out to build 'temples' to God in the search for a wider spiritual concept.[8] The ideas of the Tabernacle and of the Temple have become almost interchangeable, and it is in this spirit that Le Corbusier called the Tabernacle 'Temple' and contrasted it with a primitive hut (*The Complete Architectural Work*, vol. I, 1964, p. 21).

In our own period, the modern so-called International Style, as found in the work of the Bauhaus, Le Corbusier, Mies van der Rohe and others, lends itself by its simplicity to the resuscitation of the architectural Temple tradition for Jewish worship. A Reform 'temple' had been dedicated in Hamburg in 1818, and the twentieth-century evolution is seen in the new synagogue built by Rudolf Friedmann and Felix Ascher in Hamburg in 1931 and taken over by the Nazis in 1938. It is now the location of the North German Radio Corporation and has been trans-

*ILL. 162*

*ILL. 153*
*ILL. 154*

163

formed into a concert hall.[9] It revives the traditional division of the forecourt, entrance pavilions, bare walls, predominant entrance and flat roof. The two side pavilions of the façade add width and the only adornment on the façade is symbolic, the menorah.

ILLS. 155, 156

The rediscovery of symbolism leads to a further reflection. Coupled with the tendency towards a contemporary style and the view of the synagogue as a community centre is a new quest for symbolic distinctiveness, emphasized by the experience of the holocaust and the survival of the Jewish people. Thus, the ancient symbol of the Burning Bush, frequently found in mediaeval manuscripts, is rediscovered as a motif of architectural sculpture. It was used by the architect Percival Goodman in the synagogue at Millburn, New Jersey, in 1951, and, equally successfully, in the Beth-El Temple, Springfield, Massachusetts, in 1952. In the latter case, the use of the term 'temple' for a synagogue, frequently found in America, should be noted as, ideologically, the ideas of the Temple and of the synagogue have become closely related. The sculptors, I. Lassaw for the Beth-El Temple and H. Ferber for the Millburn Synagogue, should be remembered, as they represent a positive artistic response to the quest for religious symbolism within Jewish consciousness. Although this symbolism is nurtured by the Bible, the Temple structure itself ceases specifically to influence synagogue architecture in the United States.[10]

ILL. 157

It is significant that the German-born Jew Eric Mendelsohn (1887–1953) remained within the European context when building synagogues in the United States. The Einstein Tower near Potsdam, of 1920–21, had not lost its attraction for him; the aggressive curves remained characteristics of his style. How freely the Jewish religious symbols are interpreted is clearly seen in Eric Mendelsohn's synagogues, especially the temple in Cleveland, Ohio and the B'nai Amoona in St. Louis, Missouri (1946–50). He stated in *Letters of an Architect*: 'The dome is the temple's interior, the idea of the tent—shielding the Ark—the ancient Jewish symbol of holiness'. Re-interpretation can go no further, as the concepts of Tabernacle, Temple and synagogue are amalgamated.[11]

Similar in temperament, but not in style, was Louis I. Kahn (1901–1974), who was concerned with plastic form, light and shadow, and wall-like vertical features. His designs for the Hurva Synagogue of 1968, now under construction in Jerusalem, respond aesthetically to the vicinity of the Dome of the Rock and the Western Wall of the Temple Precincts, the so-called Wailing Wall. It is the wall combined with the vault that is the distinguishing element in the projects, and assures their monumentality. It should be remembered that Kahn also designed a simple Memorial for the Victims of the Holocaust for Battery Park in New York in 1967–69.[12]

What is it that characterizes contemporary religious art? Although modern synagogues are frequently designated as temples, especially in the United States, the influence of the Temple concept as an architectural inspiration is receding into the background. Although it persists on rare occasions, other functional tendencies make themselves felt. In the past also, synagogue architecture was influenced by contemporary styles, but an attempt was made, if not always successfully, to differentiate it from church architecture. At the present time, however, the place of religion in life is challenged, not only in Judaism but also in Christianity. The open plan, with movable partitions, stresses the social and educational aspects of religious building. The emphasis is not solely on worship, and frequently religious symbols have to explain what denomination the building serves. Differences therefore tend to be minimized, and in this *ILL. 160* context the campus of Brandeis University, Waltham, Massachusetts gives an outstanding example, as a triple arrangement of chapels, Catholic, Protestant and Jewish are clustered together. The buildings, of great similarity, are the work of Harrison and Abramowitz, dated 1954.[13]

In recent years the artistic impetus of Friedmann and Ascher's synagogue in Hamburg has been revived in Europe, where two examples can be singled out. The Bentincklaan Synagogue in Rotterdam of 1955, by *ILL. 158* J. S. Baars and J. van Duin, seems to have been inspired by the Wailing Wall and pylons, a spiritually moving and architecturally successful inspiration. At the Strasbourg Synagogue de la Paix of 1958 by Claude *ILL. 159* Mayer-Levy the exterior is adorned by a menorah with six, not seven, branches, an observance of the Talmudic prohibition to copy the one that traditionally stood in the Tabernacle and in the Temple (e.g. *Bab. Avodah Zarah* 43a, *Bab. Menahoth* 28b). The façade is articulated by two slender columns which, despite their architectural function, may vaguely suggest the two pillars, Jachin and Boaz.[14]

Looking back over the years in which the vision of the Temple was a popular religious theme, maintaining continuity whilst changing, one wonders what the future will bring. In the United States the ancient symbols have been re-interpreted freely in recent years. One resuscitated visionary expression of faith is the representation of the Burning Bush that was not consumed (*Exodus* 3: 2). Although rare in earlier periods as an iconographic motif, except in narrative manuscripts, it is now popular in synagogue decoration as it expresses faith in survival after the holocaust. Rachel Wischnitzer has thrown light on American developments, but it is surprising how dated her valuations now appear as they are orientated towards a merely functional and non-symbolic style. At present, Neo-Classical motifs and symbolic expressions are being rediscovered, and a sense of direction is now set against flexibility of spatial values.

It is in this spirit that the international teams have excavated, and are excavating, Jerusalem, in particular the Temple Mount under the direction of Professor Benjamin Mazar. Here monumental architectural features, the reconstruction of steep stairs into the valley and a massive bridge testify to the enthusiastic, if not wholly accurate, witness of Josephus.

*ILL. 161*

Archaeological discoveries have acquired an almost sacred dimension in Jerusalem. Among them is an evocative fragment of a Hebrew inscription from the south-west corner of the Temple Mount referring to 'the house of the *tekiah*', the place of sounding of a long blast, presumably by the *shofar*.[15] However, the necessity for transcendent and sublime visions is perhaps felt as strongly at the present time as ever before. Jews and Christians have been enemies, but they have also co-operated significantly. So the ancient visions may in the future act as an inspiration and a stimulant for new religious insights, still connected with revived traditional forms and ancient pieties.

*ILL. 163*

## References

1  On Chagall cf. catalogue of the *Musée National Message Biblique, Marc Chagall* (Nice 1973).

2  R. Rosenblum, *Modern Painting and the Northern Romantic Tradition, Friedrich to Rothko* (London 1975) with good illustrations but, in our view, far over-stressing the continuity of the Romantic element.

3  On Semper see H. Rosenau in the *Leo Baeck Yearbook,* vol. XXII (1977), pp. 237 ff. On historicism see L. Grote (ed.), *Historismus und Bildende Kunst* (Munich 1965).

4  Hegel's views on aesthetics in *Georg Wilhelm Friedrich Hegel's Sämtliche Werke* (Stuttgart 1927), vol. XII, especially pp. 494 ff. Hegel is intensely revealing. Without necessarily adopting his views on the one-sidedness of Judaism, one can nevertheless appreciate his deep insight into the essence of an imageless cult. On philosophy of religion, see vol. XVI (Stuttgart 1928), pp. 81 ff.; on metaphor, see D. Stewart in *Journal of Aesthetics and Art Criticism* (1973), pp. 205 ff.

5  M. Ghyka, *A Practical Handbook of Geometrical Composition and Design* (London 1952), p. 6.

6  'The Secret of the Golden Flower' in *Alchemical Studies*, vol. XIII of Jung's *Collected Works* (London 1967–68), pp. 6 ff. The figure A.10 is a mandala designed by Jung himself. The cult connected with the Ka'ba knows both circumambulation and direction (see above p. 69). Cf. A. J. Wensinck in *The Encyclopaedia of Islam, passim.*

7  On Egyptian derivations cf. Busink, pp. 566 ff., who seems over-sceptical. The sense of direction is so paramount in Egyptian temples that it may well have exerted an influence, even if it is impossible to define it clearly in detail. There is also, perhaps, an Egyptian influence in the 120 cubits stipulated for the height of the façade, as suggested above.

8  G. Scholem, *Major Trends in Jewish Mysticism* (London 1955), especially with reference to symbolism, cf. pp. 216 f. Also *The Messianic Idea in Judaism* (London

1971), pp. 257 ff. It is to be regretted that a great scholar like Professor Scholem does not show a little more tolerance to Jewish Reform Movements and their adoption of the six-pointed star as a religious symbol.

9   This synagogue was not destroyed by the Nazis, an exceptional situation. It now forms part of the buildings of the Norddeutscher Rundfunk in Hamburg.

10  Wischnitzer, *Synagogue Architecture in the United States*, pp. 146, 156 f. and *passim*. Here Baron's thoughtful emphasis on past synagogues as places for education should be remembered. Baron, *op. cit.*, vol. VII, pp. 137 ff.

11  Eric Mendelsohn, *Letters of an Architect* (ed. O. Beyer), (London 1967), especially p. 171; A. Whittick, *Eric Mendelsohn* (London 1964), pp. 146 ff. For background see A. Kampf, *Contemporary Synagogue Art* (New York 1966) and P. Thiry, R. M. Bennet and H. L. Kamphoefner, *Churches and Temples* (New York 1953), pp. J 3 ff. Also B. Zevi, *Erich Mendelsohn, Opera Completa* (Milan 1970).

12  *L'Architecture d'Aujourd'hui*, vol. 40 (1969), pp. 1 ff. and V. Scully, *Louis I. Kahn* (New York and London 1962); also L. I. Kahn, *The Notebooks and Drawings of L. I. Kahn* (Cambridge, Massachusetts 1973); R. Giurgola and J. Mehta, *L. I. Kahn* (Denver 1975).

13  P. Thiry *et al.*, *op. cit.*, *passim*.

14  Wischnitzer, *The European Synagogue*, pp. 263 and 265 ff.

15  See note 8 to Introduction.

**149** Marc Chagall, *The Song of Songs* (Nice, Musée National Message Biblique)

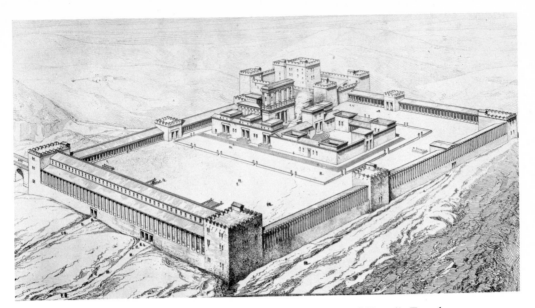

**150**  Melchior de Vogüé, *Le Temple de Jérusalem,* reconstruction of Herod's Temple

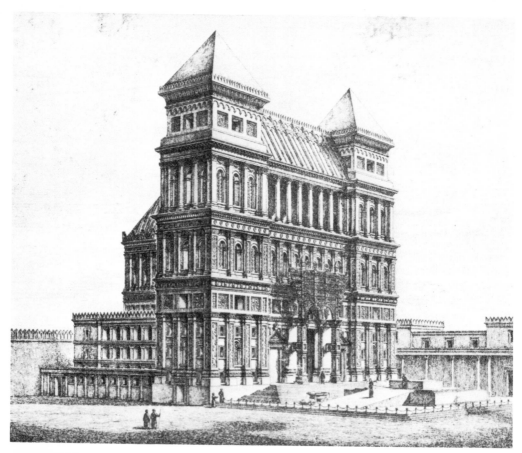

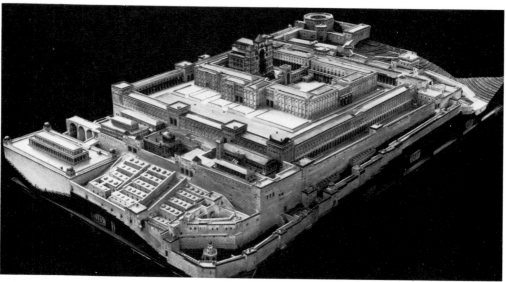

**153**  R. Friedmann and F. Ascher, Hamburg Synagogue, Oberstrasse, 1931, interior

(*opposite top*)
**151**  James Fergusson, *The Temples of the Jews* . . . , perspective view of Herod's Temple (London, British Library)

(*opposite bottom*)
**152**  C. Schick, *Die Stiftshütte, der Tempel* . . . , model of Solomon's Temple

**156**   Plaque at Hamburg Synagogue, Oberstrasse: 'This building served as a house of worship to the Israelite community of faith up to 9 November 1938' (photo, H. E. Müller)

(*opposite top*)
**154**   R. Friedmann and F. Ascher, Hamburg Synagogue, Oberstrasse, 1931, exterior

(*opposite bottom*)
**155**   Hamburg Synagogue, Oberstrasse, present state

**157** Percival Goodman, Millburn Synagogue, 1951

**158** J. S. Baars and J. van Duin, Bentincklaan Synagogue, Rotterdam, 1955

**159** Claude Mayer-Levy, Synagogue de la Paix, Strasbourg, 1958, exterior

**160** Harrison and Abramowitz, Three Chapels at Brandeis University, Waltham, Massachusetts

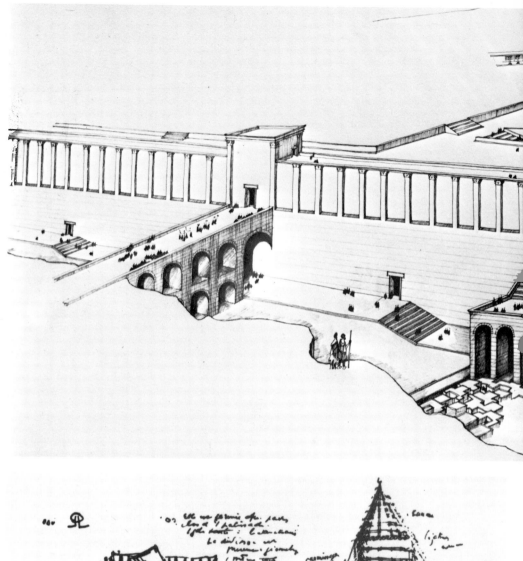

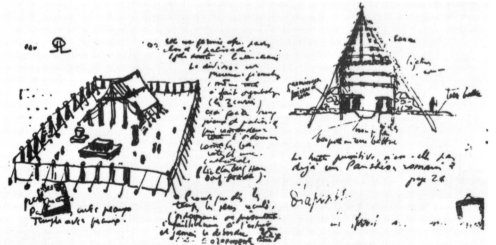

178

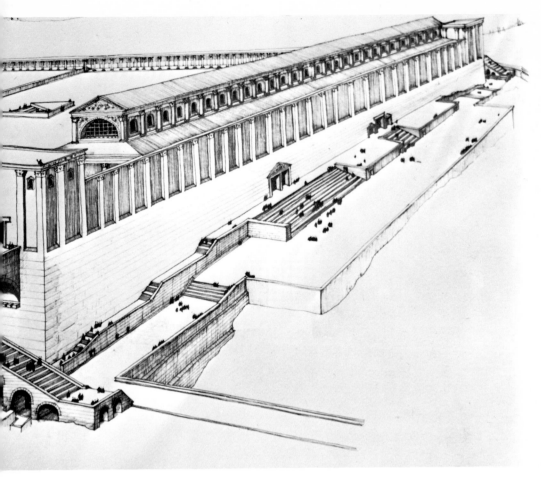

**161** B. Mazar, reconstruction of the road to the Temple Mount

(*opposite*)
**162** Le Corbusier, sketch of the Tabernacle, tent contrasted with the hut, from *The Complete Architectural Work*

**163** Hebrew inscription from the Temple Mount, Jerusalem, referring to the sounding of the *shofar* (photograph by courtesy of Israel Department of Antiquities)

**164**  El-Hanani and collaborators, Pillar of Heroism, 1970, from Memorial for Victims of the Holocaust, Jerusalem (photograph by courtesy of Israel Department of Antiquities)

# Conclusions

DESPITE THE MASS of pictorial material available, only four basic visual forms of the Temple image have survived to the present time.

The oldest is the façade of the Herodian Temple. The second, the mediaeval reconstruction of an idealized building, incorporated features both of the Solomonic and the Herodian Temples, with a special interest in the high elevation of the façade, based on II *Chronicles* 3: 4. This was followed by a free interpretation in Protestant and Catholic reconstructions, among which Villalpando's synthesis of biblical and Vitruvian thought is outstanding. Lastly the synagogue claims the succession of the Temple during the period of Emancipation, whilst the contemporary scene is full of contradictions, and no clear picture of Temple iconography is emerging.

*p. 185*

The visual image of the Temple plays only a minor, though significant, rôle in the popular biblical cycles, which deal with stories rather than abstractions. Nevertheless the Temple remains significant as it evokes a Holy House, an age-old symbol, and not a technological artefact. It thus appeals to unconscious rather than conscious motivations.

C. G. Jung's concentration on the mandala has been previously discussed. This thought has diverted attention from the main stream of Near Eastern and Western religious architecture,[1] which is characterized by the striving for a defined goal, devotional or ethical, and is opposed to the Far Eastern concepts of circularity and of the equivalence between light and darkness or good and evil.[2]

In assessing the present situation it has to be acknowledged that the Temple image has lessened in impact. It has to be remembered that already in *Revelation*, when the coming down of the New Jerusalem out of heaven is described, John saw no Temple therein (*Revelation* 21: 22). As for the majority of the Jews, the rebuilding of the Temple is not regarded as an actual possibility, and to many such a construction appears undesirable. However, images and symbols remain potent. Such a symbol is represented by the Yad Vashem, designed by Arie El-Hanani and built

*ILLS. 165, 166*

in Jerusalem from 1960. It is a memorial dedicated to the martyrs of the Holocaust and, by implication, to all innocent martyrs. The buildings include the Memorial Hall, a synagogue, archives and a section honouring the righteous gentiles. The memorial, situated on a prominent hill, is a place of pilgrimage, visited with devotion by inhabitants of many lands. The austere main centre, erected with unadorned walls and based on unhewn stones, evokes a response of awe, such as worshippers approaching the Temple had felt in the past. Buildings and monuments are being added constantly. Among them the Pillar of Heroism by B. Schwartz is out- *ILL. 164* standing.[3]

Our study seeks to demonstrate how in certain periods religious and intellectual personalities co-operated in hostile environments and in spite of this entered into amicable contacts. It is to these élites that the Temple owed the interpretation of universality,[4] and it could therefore become not only a symbol for Christians and Jews, but also a symbol for all nations. This thought is already found in the biblical prophecy (*Isaiah* 56: 7) *My house shall be called a house of prayer for all peoples.*

### References

1  C. G. Jung, *Collected Works*, especially *Psychology of the Unconscious* (numerous editions).

2  H. Rosenau, *Design and Mediaeval Architecture, op. cit.,* pp. 1 ff.; Rosenau, *The Ideal City* (2nd edn.), pp. 14 ff.; and J. Beckwith, *Early Christian and Byzantine Art* (Harmondsworth 1970), p. 3, on the influence of the Temple.

3  See entries on 'Yad Vashem' and 'Jerusalem' in the *Encyclopaedia Judaica.* Also for this and other memorials cf. A. Rieth, *Monuments to the Victims of Tyranny* (New York, Washington and London 1969). I am indebted to Mr. S. Spector, Secretary-General of Yad Vashem, for recent information.

4  Hammer-Schenk, *op. cit.,* pp. 122 ff. and *passim* gives some significant references and Wischnitzer, *Synagogue Architecture in the United States* alludes briefly to the relevant problems.

(*opposite top*)
**165**  El-Hanani and collaborators, Memorial for Victims of the Holocaust, Jerusalem, 1961, exterior view (photograph by courtesy of Israel Department of Antiquities)

(*opposite bottom*)
**166**  El-Hanani and collaborators, Memorial for Victims of the Holocaust, Jerusalem, 1961, interior (photograph by courtesy of Israel Department of Antiquities)

# Extracts from Sources

**The Holy Scriptures according to the Masoretic text**
**(Jewish Publication Society of America, 1955)**

### I KINGS   Chapter 6

1. And it came to pass in the four hundred and eightieth year after the children of Israel were come out of the land of Egypt, in the fourth year of Solomon's reign over Israel, in the month Ziv, which is the second month, that he began to build the house of the Lord. 2. And the house which king Solomon built for the Lord, the length thereof was threescore cubits, and the breadth thereof twenty cubits, and the height thereof thirty cubits. 3. And the porch before the temple of the house, twenty cubits was the length thereof, according to the breadth of the house; and ten cubits was the breadth thereof before the house. 4. And for the house he made windows broad within, and narrow without. 5. And against the wall of the house he built a side-structure round about, against the walls of the house round about, both of the temple and of the Sanctuary; and he made side chambers round about . . .

### Chapter 7

13. And king Solomon sent and fetched Hiram out of Tyre. 14. He was the son of a widow of the tribe of Naphtali, and his father was a man of Tyre, a worker in brass; and he was filled with wisdom and understanding and skill, to work all works in brass. And he came to king Solomon, and wrought all his work. 15. Thus he fashioned the two pillars of brass, of eighteen cubits high each; and a line of twelve cubits did compass it about; [and so] the other pillar. 16. And he made two capitals of molten brass, to set upon the tops of the pillars; the height of the one capital was five cubits, and the height of the other capital was five cubits.

## II CHRONICLES   Chapter 3

1. Then Solomon began to build the house of the Lord at Jerusalem in mount Moriah, where [the Lord] appeared unto David his father; for which provision had been made in the Place of David, in the threshing-floor of Ornan the Jebusite. 2. And he began to build in the second day of the second month in the fourth year of his reign. 3. Now these are the foundations which Solomon laid for the building of the house of God. The length by cubits after the ancient measure was threescore cubits, and the breadth twenty cubits. 4. And the porch that was before [the house], the length of it, according to the breadth of the house, was twenty cubits, and the height a hundred and twenty; and he overlaid it within with pure gold. 5. And the greater house he covered with cypress-wood, which he overlaid with fine gold, and wrought thereon palm-trees and chains. 6. And he garnished the house with precious stones for beauty; and the gold was gold of Parvaim. 7. He overlaid also the house, the beams, the thresholds, and the walls thereof, and the doors thereof, with gold; and graved cherubim on the walls . . .

15. Also he made before the house two pillars of thirty and five cubits high, and the capital that was on the top of each of them was five cubits.

## Josephus:   THE JEWISH WAR

*Translation from Excursus VI by G. A. Williamson (Penguin Books, 1959).*

No foreigner was to enter the Sacred Precincts – this was the name given to the second court. Fourteen steps led up to it from the first: the elevated area was rectangular and had a protecting wall of its own. The height of this on the outside was sixty feet, but it was concealed by the steps: on the inside it was only thirty-seven and a half feet. For the interior was perched up at the top of the steps and so could not all be seen, concealed as it was by being higher up the hill. Beyond the fourteen steps there was a space of fourteen feet to the wall, quite flat. From there other flights of five steps led up to the gates. On the north and south the gates numbered eight, four in each case; on the east there were bound to be two, for on this side a special place was walled off for the women to worship in, necessitating a second gate, which opened facing the first. On the other sides there was one north and one south gate through which the Court of the Women could be entered; for through the others women were not admitted, nor might they go by their own gate past the dividing wall. This court was open for worship alike to native women and to Jewesses from abroad. The western part had no gate at all, there being no openings in the wall on that side. The colonnades between the gates faced inwards from the wall in front of the treasury, and rested on pillars of exceptional height and beauty; they were single, but apart from size were in every way equal to those round the lower court.

The Sanctuary itself, the Holy Temple, situated in the middle, was reached by a flight of twelve steps. Seen from the front it was of the same height and width, each 150 feet, but behind it was sixty feet narrower, for the entrance was flanked by shoulders, as it were, projecting thirty feet on either side. The first gate was 105 feet high and thirty-seven and a half wide; it had no doors, symbolizing thus the vast, inexclusible expanse of heaven. The face was covered with gold all over, and through the arch the first chamber could all be seen from without, huge as it was, and the inner gate and its surrounding wall, all glistening with gold, struck the beholder's eye. The Sanctuary was divided into two chambers, but only the first was visible, all the way up, as it rose 135 feet from the ground, its length being seventy-five and its width thirty. The gate of this was, as I said, covered with gold all over, as was the entire wall surrounding it. Above it were the golden grape-vines, from which hung bunches as big as a man. The Sanctuary was two storeys high and so appeared lower inside than outside. There were golden doors $82\frac{1}{2}$ feet high and 24 wide. In front of these was a curtain of the same length, Babylonian tapestry embroidered with blue, scarlet, linen thread, and purple, a marvellous example of the craftsman's art. The mixture of materials had a clear mystic meaning, typifying all creation: it seemed that scarlet symbolized fire, linen the earth, blue the air, and purple the sea. In two cases the resemblance was one of colour; in the linen and purple it was a question of origin, as the first comes from the earth, the second from the sea. Worked in the tapestry was the whole vista of the heavens except for the signs of the Zodiac.

**Tractate of the Mishnah, the Babylonian Talmud** (*Soncino Press, 1948*)

## MIDDOTH   Chapter II

*Mishnah* 1. The temple mount was five hundred cubits by five hundred. The greater part of it was on the south; next to that on the east; next to that on the north; and the smallest part on the west. The part which was most extensive was the part most used.

## MIDDOTH   Chapter IV

*Mishnah* 6. The hekal was a hundred cubits by a hundred with a height of a hundred. The substructure was six cubits, then it rose forty, then a cubit for the ornamentation, two cubits for the guttering, a cubit for the roof and a cubit for the plastering. The height of the upper chamber was forty cubits, there was a cubit for its ornamentation, two cubits for the guttering, a cubit for the ceiling, a cubit for the plastering, three cubits for the parapet and a cubit for the spikes. R. Judah says the spikes were not included in the measurement, the parapet being four cubits.

*Mishnah* 7. From east to west was a hundred cubits – the wall of the porch five cubits, the porch itself eleven, the wall of the hekal six cubits and its interior forty, a cubit for the partition and twenty cubits for the Holy of Holies, the wall of the hekal six cubits, the cell six cubits and the wall of the cell five. From north to south was seventy cubits – the wall of the mesibbah five cubits, the mesibbah itself three, the wall of the cell five and the cell itself six, the wall of the hekal six cubits and its interior twenty, then the wall of the hekal again six and the cell six and its wall five, then the place of the water descent three cubits and its wall five cubits. The porch extended beyond this fifteen cubits on the north and fifteen cubits on the south, and this space was called the knifehouse where they used to store the [slaughterers'] knives. Thus the hekal was narrow behind and broad in front, resembling a lion, as it says, ah, Ariel, Ariel, the city where David encamped. Just as a lion is narrow behind and broad in front, so the hekal was narrow behind and broad in front.

# Select Bibliography

**Works of Reference and Encyclopaedias:**

*Encyclopaedia Judaica.* Jerusalem 1971–72.

*The Jewish Encyclopedia.* New York and London 1925.

Mayer, L.A., *Bibliography of Jewish Art.* Jerusalem 1967.

*Monumenta Judaica, 2000 Jahre Geschichte und Kultur der Juden am Rhein*, vol. 2: *Handbuch.* Cologne 1963.

Thieme, U. and Becker, F., *Allgemeines Lexikon der bildenden Künstler von der Antike bis zur Gegenwart.* Leipzig 1907 etc.

**Recommended Books:**

Baron, I. W., *A Social and Religious History of the Jews.* New York 1952 etc.

Busink, T. A., *Der Tempel von Jerusalem von Salomo bis Herodes*. Leiden 1970.

Frankl, P., *The Gothic*. Princeton 1960.

Fraser, D., Hibbard, H. and Lewine, M. J. (eds.), *Essays Presented to Rudolf Wittkower*. London 1967.

Goodenough, E. R., *Jewish Symbols in the Greco-Roman Period*. New York 1953–65.

Hammer-Schenk, H., *Untersuchungen zum Synagogenbau in Deutschland 1800–1871*. Tübingen 1974.

Hollis, F. J., *The Archaeology of Herod's Temple*. London 1934.

Kubler, G. and Soria, M., *Art and Architecture in Spain and Portugal*. Harmondsworth 1959.

Leveen, J., *The Hebrew Bible in Art*. London 1944.

Nordström, C. O., 'The Duke of Alba's Castilian Bible', *Figura,* n.s. vol. V (1967).

Rosenau, H., *A Short History of Jewish Art*. London 1948.

Rosenau, H., *The Ideal City: its Architectural Evolution*. (2nd edn.) London 1974.

Rosenblum, R., *Modern Painting and the Northern Romantic Tradition*. London 1975.

Sukenik, E. L., *The Ancient Synagogue of Beth Alpha*. Jerusalem and Oxford 1932.

Sukenik, E. L., *Ancient Synagogues in Palestine and Greece*. London 1934.

Wischnitzer, R., *The Architecture of the European Synagogue*. Philadelphia 1964.

Wischnitzer, R., *Synagogue Architecture in the United States: History and Interpretation*. Philadelphia 1955.

Further bibliographical references will be found in the footnotes to each chapter.

# Index

Aaron   21
Abraham   92
Abramowitz, Max   165, 176, 177
Adam, James   95, 139
Adam, Robert   95, 139
Adelphi (London)   95
*Afbeeldingen der merkwaardisgte Geschiedenissen van het Oude en Nieuwe Testament . . .* (Luyken)   96, 116
*Afbeeldinghe van den Tempel Salomonis* (Templo)   132, 133
Agrippa   134
al-Aksa mosque (Jerusalem)   65
Alberti, Leone Battista   92, 104
Alembert, Jean d'   93
Altar of Hewn Stone   92
*Antiquitatum Iudaicarum* (Montanus)   94
*Antiquités Judaïques* (Josephus)   66, 82, 83, 84, 85
*Apparatus Biblicus* (Lamy)   98, 128, 129
*Architectura Civil Recta y Obliqua* (Caramuel von Lobkowitz)   134, 141(3), 143
*architecture et art de bien bastir, L'* (Alberti)   92, 104
Arnauld, Antoine   97
Ascher, Felix   163, 165, 171, 172, 173

Baars, Jacob S.   165, 174
Bar Kochba   20, 21, 23, 24, 28, 33
Bechhofen, Synagogue of   66, 136
Bede, St.   38, 40

Bentincklaan Synagogue (Rotterdam)   165, 174
Bernard of Clairvaux, St.   25(11), 37
Bernini, Gian Lorenzo   67
Beth-Alpha, Synagogue of   23
Beth-El Temple (Springfield)   164
Beth-Elohim Synagogue (Charleston)   139, 156
Beth-She'an, Synagogue of   23, 30
*Bible Historiale* (Desmoulins)   38, 55
B'nai Amoona (St. Louis)   164
Boisserée, Sulpice   66, 80,81
Borbonius, Nicolaus   68
Bordeaux, Synagogue of   138, 142(17), 152, 153
Bordes, Auguste   142(17)
Borromini, Francesco   96, 118
Brandeis University (Waltham)   165, 176, 177
Breydenbach, Bernhard von   65, 74
Brosse, Salomon de   93
Bundy, Richard   98, 128, 129
Burak, El   69

Calvin, John   92
Caramuel von Lobkowitz, Juan   134, 141(3), 143
Castro, Leon de   94
Chagall, Marc   161, 168
Charenton, Temple of   93, 94, 105
*Charge of St. Peter, The* (Perugino)   68, 86
Charles William Ferdinard,

Duke of Brunswick   137
*Chronology of Ancient Kingdoms Amended* (Newton)   97, 123
Claudius, Emperor of Rome   28
*Code Napoléon*   136
Cologne, Cathedral of   66
Coloors, Father Andreas de   65, 70
Colosseum (Rome) · 73
Comestor, Petrus   37, 54
*Commentary* [to *Kings*] (Rashi)   40
*Commentary* [to *Middoth*] (Maimonides)   42
Compiègne de Veil, Louis   92, 135, 136
Conduitt, John   97
Corcelles, Arnaud   138, 152, 153
Court of the Israelites   15
Court of the Women   15
*Crucifixion, The* (attr. Barend van Orley)   73

David, King of Judah and Israel   14, 40, 97, 141(8), 163
'*David and Absalom'* (Rembrandt)   68, 86, 136, 141(8)
Decastro, M. P.   134, 135
*Description of the Temple of Solomon* (Newton)   97
Delamonce, Ferdinand   98, 99
Desbrulins, F.   99
Desmoulins, Guyart   38, 55
*Dictionnaire universel*   93
Diderot, Denis   93
Dohm, Christian Wilhelm   137
Dome of the Grail   66, 80, 81

Dome of the Rock (Jerusalem) 14, 15, 16, 64, 65, 66, 68, 69, 92, 136, 161, 164
Duin, Jan van 165, 174
Dura-Europos, Synagogue of 2, 20, 21, 22, 23, 24, 29, 33, 37
Durand, Charles 142(17)
Düsseldorf Synagogue 137, 138, 150

Einstein Tower (Potsdam) 164
El-Hanani, Arie 180, 181, 182, 183
Eliezer ben Jacob 19
Elijah 68
Ellies Du Pin, Louis 97, 98
*Encyclopédie* 93
*Entwürff einer Historischen Architectur* (Fischer von Erlach) 97, 118, 119
Escorial 94, 95, 112, 113, 134, 143
Estienne Bible 91, 92
Eupolemos 15
*Exemplar siue de sacris fabricis liber* (Montanus) 94, 107, 108, 109, 110
Eyck, Hubert van 64, 65
*Ezechielem Explanationes, In* (Prado and Villalpando) 94, 95, 111, 112, 114, 115
Ezekiel 34, 36, 38, 39, 43, 95, 135, 159

Farhi Bible 37
Ferber, Herbert 164
Fergusson, James 161, 170, 171
*figures du Temple et du palais de Salomon, Les* (Maillet) 99, 129, 130, 131
Fischer von Erlach, Johann Bernhard 97, 118, 119
Flaminius, Leo *see* Rauwolf, Leonhard
*fortifications et artifices, Des* (Perret) 93, 105
Fortress Antonia (Jerusalem) 132, 134, 135
Foucquet, Jean 66, 67, 82, 83, 84, 85
Frauenkirche (Munich) 67
Friedmann, Rudolf 163, 165, 171, 172, 173
Furetière, Antoine 93

*Géographie sacrée* (Sanson) 99
Gerondi, Jonah ben Abraham 66
*Geschichte des Jüdischen Volkes* (Dohm) 137
*Glossa Ordinaria* 38
Goethe, Johann Wolfgang von 66, 140
Goodman, Percival 164, 174
Great Synagogue (London) 94, 139, 155
Grégoire, Henri 136
*Gudea* 19, 27

Hadrian, Emperor of Rome 20
Hafenreffer, Matthias 93, 106
Haggadah, Amsterdam 135, 146
Haggadah of Sarajevo 24, 25(17), 36, 37, 41, 52
Haggadah, Venice 66, 74
Hall of Hewn Stone 35, 98
Hamburg Synagogue 163, 164, 165, 167(9), 171, 172, 173
Hammam-Lif, Synagogue of 17
Haninah ben Hezekiah 38
*Hannah Teaching Samuel* (Rembrandt) 68, 136, 148
Harrison, Peter 165, 176, 177
*Healing of the Lame at the Beautiful Gate, The* (Raphael) 67, 85
Hegel, Georg Wilhelm Friedrich 162, 166(4)
Herod I, King of Judea 15, 16, 17, 19, 20, 21, 38, 67, 92, 169, 170, 171
Herrera, Juan de 95, 112, 113
Hiram of Tyre 34
*Historia Scholastica* (Comestor) 37, 54
*Historiarum Veteris Testamenti Icones* etc. 68
Holbein, Hans, the younger 68, 85
Hollar, Wenzel 96
Holy Sepulchre (Jerusalem) 65, 66, 92
Horb, Synagogue of 66, 77, 136
Houghton Chapel 161
Hurva Synagogue (Jerusalem) 164
Huyberts, Cornelis 96, 100(13), 120

Huygens, Christian 135, 141(4)

*Icones Bibliae* (Merian) 135, 146, 147
*Iggeret ha-Teshuvah* (Gerondi) 66
*Introduction à l'écriture sainte* (Lamy) 98, 127
Israels, Joseph 136
Isserlein, Israel 66, 73
*Itinerarium per Palaestinam* (Rauwolf) 96, 117

Jachin and Boaz 15, 23, 44(3), 91, 96, 97, 98, 138, 165
Jachin and Booz (Würzburg) 34
Jacob, Abraham ben 135, 146
*Jacobi Jehudae Leonis de Templo Hierosolomytano* (Templo) 134
Jacobson, Israel 137
Jacobson, Jacob 137
Jacobstempel (Seesen) 137
Jaucourt, Louis, Chevalier de 93
Jerome Bonaparte, King of Westphalia 136
Jesus Christ 71, 94, 109, 117
*Jewish Bride, The* (Rembrandt) 141(8)
*Jewish War, The* (Josephus) 19, 42, 134
John, St. 181
Jonathan 141(8)
Joseph II, Holy Roman Emperor 137
Josephus 15, 19, 42, 66, 134, 166
Joshua 33
Joshuah ben Abraham ben Gaon 35
Jud (Leu), Johannes 91, 92
Juda (Judä), Leo 91
Judah ben Tema, Rabbi 17
Julian 'the Apostate', Emperor of Rome 16
Jung, Carl Gustav 163, 166(6), 181

Ka'ba (Mecca) 69, 89, 166(6)
Kahn, Louis I 164
Karlsruhe Synagogue 137, 138, 151
Khirbet-Susiiya, Synagogue of 22, 23, 30

Kimche, David  38, 40, 95, 133
Kirchheim, Synagogue of  66, 77, 136
Klees-Wuelbern, Johann Heinrich  139, 156
Knights Templar  65, 70, 92
Koberger, Anton  39, 41, 65
Koehler, Peter  137
Krahe, Peter  137, 138, 150

Lamy, Bernard  97, 98, 124, 125, 126, 127, 129
Landesherr, Andreas 139
Lassaw, Ibram  164
Le Corbusier (Charles-Edouard Jeanneret)  163, 178, 179
Ledoux, Claude-Nicolas  137, 138
L'Empereur, Constantin  96, 97, 122, 134
Leon, Jacob Judah (Aryeh) *see* Templo
*Letters of an Architect* (Mendelsohn)  164
Leu, Johannes *see* Jud, Johannes
*Liber Cronicarum* (Schedel)  41, 65, 71
Liberius, Pope St.  16
Liebermann, Max  136
Lopez, David  139, 156
Louis XIV, King of France  99
Louvre (Paris)  92
Luyken (Luiken), Jan (Johannes)  96, 116

Maillet, Louis  98, 99, 129, 130, 131
Maimonides (Moses ben Maimon)  35, 36, 38, 42, 43, 48, 73, 92, 136
Maimunah  69
Malebranche, Nicolas  97
Marot, Jean  105
Martin, Jean  92, 104
Mayer-Levy, Claude  165, 175
Mazar, Benjamin  166, 178, 179
Memorial for Victims of the Holocaust (Jerusalem) *see* Yad Vashem
Memorial for the Victims of the Holocaust (New York)  164
Mendelsohn, Eric  164
Mendelssohn, Moses  136, 137

Merian, Matthaeus, the elder  96, 135, 146, 147
Métivier, Jean-Baptiste  139
Mies van der Rohe, Ludwig  163
Millburn Synagogue  164, 174
*Mischna* (Surenhusius edition)  96, 120, 121, 134
*Mishnah Commentary* (Maimonides)  35, 48
*Mishneh Torah* (Maimonides)  35, 48, 92, 98, 104
*Mishneh Torah,* Frankfurt (Maimonides)  66, 73
Mohammed  69, 89
Montanus, Benedictus Arias  42, 94, 95, 107, 108, 109, 110
Moses  22, 33, 68, 91
Moullart-Sanson, Pierre  99

Na'aran, Synagogue of  17
Napoleon I Bonaparte, Emperor of France  136, 137
Nebuzar-Adan  70
New Israelitic Synagogue (Hamburg)  139, 156
Newton, Isaac  97, 123
Nicolaus de Lyra  23, 39, 40, 41, 42, 43, 45(25), 56, 57, 59, 60, 61, 62, 63, 65, 67, 68, 69(10), 94
Noah  94, 98, 109

*Origin of Building or the Plagiarism of the Heathens Detected, The* (Wood)  140, 156, 157, 158, 159
Orley, Barend van  73

Palazzo Publico (Siena)  22
Pantheon (Rome)  14
Paul of Burgos (Paul de Santa Maria *or* Solomon ha Levi)  42
Pecht, Friedrich  162
Pentateuch, Ashburnham  32, 33
Pentateuch, Copenhagen  36, 51
Pentateuch, Hebrew  33, 44(3)
Pentateuch, Paris  36, 51
*Peregrinatio in Terram Sanctam* (Breydenbach)  65, 74
Perrault, Claude  92, 104, 135
Perret, Jacques  93, 105, 134
Perugino  68, 86

Philip II, King of Spain  94
Philo of Alexandria  22, 24
Picard, Bernard  98
Pillar of Heroism (Jerusalem)  180, 182
Pine, Jacob  98
Polyglot Bible  94
Pompey  67, 85
*Portraict du Temple de Salomon* (Templo)  133
Portuguese Synagogue (Amsterdam)  94, 135
Portuguese Synagogue (London)  94
*Postillae* (Nicolaus de Lyra)  39, 40, 41, 56, 57, 59, 60, 61, 62, 63, 65
Prado, Hieronymo  94
*Presentation of the Christ Child* (Rembrandt)  136, 149
Ptolemy I Soter, King of Egypt  66, 82
Pugin, Augustus Welby  155

Raphael  67, 68, 85, 86
Rashi (Rabbi Solomon ben Isaac)  23, 34, 38, 40, 42, 43, 133
Rauwolf, Leonhard  96, 117
*Re Aedificatoria, De* (Alberti)  92
Rembrandt van Rijn  68, 86, 136, 141(8), 148, 149, 162
*Responsa* (Rashi)  34
*Retrato del Templo de Selomoh* (Templo)  132, 133, 134, 144
Reuwich, Erhard  65
Richard of St. Victor  36, 50
Rothko, Mark  161
Royal College (Paris)  91
Rue Notre-Dame-de-Nazareth, Temple of the (Paris)  138, 139, 154, 155, 160, 162

St. Charles Borromaeus, Church of (Vienna)  97, 118, 119
Saint Martin-ès-Vignes, Church of (Troyes)  99
St. Peter's (Rome)  67
Saladin, Sultan of Egypt and Syria  35
Sandrié, P. J.  138, 142(18), 154, 155
Sankt Gallen  33

Sanson, Nicolas  99
Sant' Ivo della Sapienza,
University Church of (Rome)
96, 118
Santa Maria Maggiore, Church
of (Rome)  16
Saubert, Johann  134
Schedel, Hartmann  41, 65, 71,
117
Schick, Conrad von  162, 170,
171
Schott, Gerhard  135, 145
Schwäbisch-Hall, Synagogue of
66, 77, 136
Schwartz, B.  182
Scotin, Gérard the elder  99
Semper, Gottfried  139, 160,
162
Silveyra, Jacob  138, 154, 155
Sistine Chapel (Rome)  68
Sixtus IV, Pope  68
Solomon, King of Judah and
Israel  14, 15, 19, 21, 26, 34, 36,
39, 40, 67, 91, 92, 93, 95, 96, 97,
99, 123, 124, 125, 127, 129, 130,
131, 132, 134, 135, 140, 146, 147,
159, 170, 171
Solomon ben Israel, Rabbi see
Rashi
Solomon ben Raphael  36
Song of Songs, The (Chagall)
161, 168
Spiller, James  139, 155
Sposalizio (Perugino)  68, 86
Sposalizio (Raphael)  68, 86, 87
Stiftshütte, der Tempel in
Jerusalem und der Tempelplatz
Jetztzeit, Die (Schick)  161, 162,
170, 171
Stil, Der (Semper)  162

Stobi, Synagogue of  17
Study of Stonehenge (Wood)
140
Surenhusius, Gulielmus  96,
120, 121, 122, 134
Sussmann ben Solomon Katz,
Eliezer  66, 136
Synagogue de la Paix
(Strasbourg)  165, 175

Tabernaculo Foederis, de sancta
Civitate Jerusalem et de Templo
ejus, De (Lamy)  97, 124, 125,
126
Temple de Jérusalem, Le
(Vogüé)  161, 169
Temples of the Jews and Other
Buildings, The (Fergusson)  161,
170, 171
Templo (Jacob Judah [Aryeh]
Leon)  36, 97, 132, 133, 134,
135, 141(3,4), 143, 144
Templo Salomonis Liber, De
(Bede)  38, 40
Templum Ezechielis (Hafenreffer)
93, 106
Terumat ha-Deshen (Isserlein)
66, 73
Theotokos Chapel (Mount
Nebo)  23
Three Marys at the Open
Sepulchre, The (attr. Hubert van
Eyck)  64
Titurel (Boisserée)  80, 81
Titus, Arch of (Rome)  6, 21, 67
Tours, Cathedral of  67
Trent, Council of  94
Troyes, Cathedral of  99
Tübingen University (Tübingen)
93

Ur, Standard of  22

Vatablus, Franciscus  91, 92,
100, 101, 102, 103, 135
Via Montana, catacomb of the
(Rome)  22
Vigna Rondanini, catacomb of
the (Rome)  22
Villalpando, Juan Bautista  94,
95, 96, 97, 98, 111, 112, 114, 115,
133, 135, 141(4), 163, 181
Visionem Ezekielis, In (Richard
of St. Victor)  36, 50
Vitruvius  94, 95, 140, 156, 157,
163
Voltz, Johann Michael  151
Vogüé, Charles Jean Melchior
de  161, 169

Wagner, Peter  151
Wailing Wall (Jerusalem)  164,
165
Weinbrenner, Friedrich  137,
138, 151
Weltchronik see Liber
Cronicarum (Schedel)
Wilhelm Meister's Travels
(Goethe)  66
Wood, John, the elder  140, 156
157, 158, 159
Worms Synagogue  34, 35, 47
Wren, Christopher  135, 141(4)
Würzburg, Cathedral of  34, 46
Wyatt, James  139

Yad Vashem (Jerusalem)  180,
181, 182, 183

Zerubbabel, Governor of
Jerusalem  15, 19, 38
Zwingli, Ulrich  91